THE WORLD'S MOST
DARING
VAGABONDS AND
VILLAINS

THE WORLD'S MOST
DARING VAGABONDS AND VILLAINS

BY

NIGEL BLUNDELL

SUNBURST BOOKS

This edition published 1996 by Sunburst Books,
Kiln House, 210 New Kings Road,
London SW6 4NZ

ISBN 1 85778 155 4

Printed and bound in Great Britain

Contents

Vagabonds and Villains

They're the crafty crooks who, when it comes to crime, think BIG. For them, acquiring wealth or notoriety means leading a life which most of us can only secretly envy.

They may be vagabonds, they may be villains, but their exploits are often remembered long after their more virtuous victims are forgotten. It is not so much what they do – but the way that they do it.

As Robert Louis Stevenson said: 'The Devil, depend upon it, can sometimes do a very gentlemanly thing'.

The characters gathered together in this book have all proved themselves to be less than ladies or gentlemen. They may not be honourable or honest. Indeed, in some cases their activities are quite reprehensible.

Yet these nefarious deeds – whether dark, deceitful or dastardly – are often the very essence of enterprise and adventure.

You may not condone them – but in many ways you just have to admire them!

DANIEL FARIES

For a multi-million dollar business, the chairman's office at headquarters was not impressive. There was no big desk, no plushly upholstered chair, no polished conference table – just cheap furniture, curtainless windows, bare walls and a single well-used telephone. But security was tight. Boss Daniel Faries was guarded night and day as he made his fortune on that telephone – from inside his very prison cell!

The battered black telephone was the key to one of the most fantastic frauds in history. It was all he needed while he let his fingers do the stealing.

As he awaited trial for murder, Danny's phone in his cell was seldom silent. Thanks to the oversight and generosity of Florida's prison service, he made a fortune from defrauding credit card owners.

He would use other people's credit cards to order goods and services for accomplices on the outside, for his fellow jailbirds, for himself – even for his prison guards. His business, which became known among Miami villains as the 'Jailhouse Shopping Network', boomed to the tune of $3 million.

Danny Faries' business has since been closed down. Danny himself was forced to move his 'premises' across the state to a high-security jail.

There he was able to regale the fellow inmates with stories about how simple it was to make a mint while in the clink.

From his new (normally phone-free) cell, he said: 'What I did was not really so smart. If they put you in a room the size of a bathroom for years at a time with only a telephone, you come up with some pretty inventive stuff – because everything you do, you do through the phone.

'I feel like I constructed a train, and just darn near anybody can drive a train. You don't have to be terribly intelligent and only marginally capable. Heck, it's on a track. All you have to do is put in the fuel – credit card numbers – and this train'll go!'

This, then, is the story of Daniel Faries, con man extraordinary, who made and gave away a fortune.

Faries had always been a petty crook, and not an expert one at that. He spent most of his adult life in Houses of Correction – and they didn't do much to correct him. When he wasn't behind bars he was leaning on them, getting drunk. And when he wasn't drunk he was drying out.

In March 1986 Danny was half-way through a course of treatment at a clinic in Jacksonville, northern Florida, when he decided to go back on the booze in a big way. A pal was having a party down in the fleshpots of Miami, so Danny broke out, stole a van and high-tailed it to where the action was.

It was some party. After two days' solid drinking, the shindig degenerated into arguments and brawls. Danny said later that someone handed him a gun and for some reason, he still can't remember why, he shot his old pal three times in the head. Surprisingly, he survived. But hours later, when police raided the house and found the trappings of drug-taking, the injured man was questioned and taken to hospital.

The following evening, police were again called to the house, where they found Danny in the backyard, unconscious and reeking of booze. In the waistband of his trousers was the gun. Several strong cups of coffee later, Danny confessed to the crime. Unfortunately his buddy died in hospital two months later and Danny found himself charged with first degree murder.

The wheels of North American justice turn exceeding slowly. For four years Danny was locked up in Dade County Jail awaiting trial. They proved to be the most lucrative years of his life – and one long nightmare for credit card holders across the USA.

Danny shared a dormitory-style cell with up to 30 fellow inmates and, because they were all on remand, they had access to a telephone in the cell. As it says in the Florida Administrative Code, detailed in section 33-8.009 (9): 'Each inmate shall be provided with reasonable access to a telephone at reasonable times'.

Danny Faries was in business.

First he phoned his pals and told them to go 'Dumpster Diving' – underworld slang for rummaging around in skips and rubbish bins looking for discarded credit card slips. Danny knew how careless people could be with their carbon receipts, which contain the name and number of the cardholder. Armed with the numbers from his 'divers', Danny would then phone the credit card companies pretending to be a retailer checking on a sale. Thinking it was a genuine inquiry, the company would give him the address and the credit limit of the card holder.

Danny would then call, say, a hi-fi company and order their most expensive model, paying over the phone with the credit card details he had just been given. In case the firm checked, he would ask the hi-fi to be delivered to the card holder's real address at a particular time. Danny would then call his 'diver' with details of the purchase, the time it was to be delivered and the name and address of the card holder.

At the appointed hour, the 'diver' would hang around outside the address. When the delivery van drew up, he would saunter over and say: 'Hey! I'm Mr So-and-so. That's my new hi-fi you've got there. Thanks a lot'. He would sign for the package, wait until the van had driven off, then head straight for the city where any one of a thousand 'fences' would give him hard cash for the goods.

The downside came to the thousands of shocked credit card holders who would look at their statements every month and discover they had bought a new TV, a slap-up meal at a top restaurant, an airline ticket to South America or a new Armani suit – courtesy of Danny Faries and his amazing jailhouse shopping fraud.

The scam worked like a dream. From his 'office' in cell 10 B3 of Dade County Jail, Danny was becoming – on paper – a very rich man.

Sometimes, if he wasn't sure of an address, he would have goods delivered to the jail itself. The stores and card companies never checked — although the delivery drivers and prison guards must have raised an eyebrow at the high-class merchandise passing through the prison gates. Danny and his fellow inmates soon became the best-dressed convicts in America, wearing designer jogging suits and the flashest of jewellery.

'Oh, yes sir, I had a "bumper" business', Faries told a jail visitor. 'It's so easy to find confederates. I never took more than half. I split half with everybody. I got robbed a lot but you just take it on the chin. Heck, it's all free'.

Even when credit card companies began to abandon the idea of carbon receipts, Danny had an answer. He formed a network of crooked sales assistants at shops, bars and restaurants and paid them $20 a piece for every card number they gave him. He would get his team to ask the cardholders to jot down their addresses and phone numbers so they could 'check the card's authenticity'

Grateful cardholders were happy to oblige, impressed at such security measures which could prevent their precious cards falling into the wrong hands. Little did they know that the information they were providing would be relayed by phone to a cell block in Dade County Jail.

Danny was beginning to look upon himself as a Robin Hood character. He reasoned that the smart card holder, after the initial shock of seeing an outrageously high statement at the end of the month, would promptly contact the authorities and have any offending items struck from the bill. It would be the profit-bloated card companies who would ultimately pick up the tab.

Danny's Jailhouse Shopping Company branched out into the world of philanthropy. He used the stolen credit card numbers to pledge thousands of dollars to charity: starving children, the homeless, the sick and the aged – all from the phone in cell 10 B3.

More in his own interests, he also ordered presents for his cellmates and their relatives. If it was 'Fingers' Joe's wedding anniversary and Fingers wouldn't be able to make the celebrations because he was locked up for six months on a theft charge,

Danny would make sure that Mrs Fingers got a nice bunch of roses and a set of ear-rings, courtesy of some poor unsuspecting guy's credit card.

Danny later claimed that his guards also got their fair share of his ill-gotten largesse. 'All the correctional officers knew what I was doing', he said. 'Their families knew what I was doing because they were receiving gifts on every holiday, birthday and anniversary'.

'They're just working stiffs', Faries told a CBS television newsman. 'They're not making much money, and they're seeing all this stuff going on. They're hearing about Dom Perignon champagne and trips to the Caribbean. So I try to send things at Christmas and on holidays'.

The interviewer then asked Faries what this arrangement cost the guards. He replied: 'Oh No! Perish the thought. No sir!'

Jail officials naturally deny accusations about gifts from Faries. But there was talk of his generosity towards charities. Danny's explanation was that, with nothing to do in his cell but watch television, he would see reports of famine and hunger and would immediately get on the phone to pledge a credit card donation. He reckoned that if the victims of his frauds had actually seen the television pictures of famine victims themselves, they'd have made the donation anyway.

The first hiccup in this otherwise smooth operation came in September 1987 when Danny, ever generous with other people's money, decided to hold a party for a group of fellow inmates who were all being released at the same time. Using the credit card number of a certain unsuspecting Dr Felix Entwhistle, Danny booked a suite at the luxurious Mayfair House Hotel in downtown Miami.

From his cell, the unselfish Danny ordered the best champagne and wall-to-wall call girls for his newly-freed chums. And all night they toasted the eponymous Dr Entwhistle, whose Gold Card was making the evening possible.

By midnight, however, a hawk-eyed member of the hotel staff, perhaps concerned at the quality of the guests (they hardly looked like a convention of eminent physicians) decided to check on the good Dr Entwhistle's credit limit. It amounted to the princely sum of $2,500 – which by then had been well and truly spent. The hotel employee found a sober member of the raucous party and suggested that credit had run out.

A phone call was made and within minutes an indignant 'Dr Entwhistle' was on the telephone to the hotel's night manager, furious at the treatment of his guests. The credit limit was immediately extended by the fawning night manager, who apologised for spoiling the doctor's party.

Some weeks later the real Dr Entwhistle was speaking just as indignantly on the phone to his credit card company.

Following his complaint, Detective Raul Ubieta of the Metro-Dade Police visited the Mayfair House to discover that no-one, genuinely, could remember who had signed the bill as the party wound up. There was, however, a hotel record of a phone call made from the suite that night. It was a local number: 5454494.

Detective Ubieta dialled the number – and got the Dade County Jail cell 10 B3.

The game appeared to be up for Danny. A special Metro-Dade police investigation unit, headed by Lieutenant Ross Hughes and fellow officer Raul Ubieta, moved in on the Jailhouse Shopping Company. They bugged the phone in Danny's cell and recorded all numbers dialled. Ubieta was stunned by the result.

'We'd never seen anything like this', he said. 'He was making orders all over the place for everybody — airline tickets, video equipment, computers, clothes. The hours he worked were outrageous.'

Sometimes police noticed a sharp decrease in the number of calls. They were worried that Danny might have smelled a rat. But an informant would tell them that the 'Managing Director' of the Jailhouse Shopping Company was high on drugs. Danny had simply taken a day off.

Ubieta and his team would try to intercept the goods Danny had just ordered over the phone. 'I'd call the suppliers and point out to them they had just been the victims of a fraud', said Ubieta. 'Many of them got angry and said that the card was genuine, and that they had checked the address and phone number. They were furious that they were losing trade. I never mentioned to them that the number belonged to Dade County Jail. They would never have believed me.'

Police evidence against Danny was building up nicely when, within weeks, their case collapsed around their ears. The Dade County Department of Corrections, who understandably had not been informed of the police investigation since some of their officers were on uncomfortably close terms with Danny, organised a search of cell 10 B3.

They found 300 stolen credit card numbers, with names, addresses, phone numbers and credit limits, requests for merchandise and even the scribbled text of messages to go with flowers ordered over the phone. For instance: 'Dear Mom – Here's wishing you a happy Mother's Day – Your loving Son'.

Police were furious at the cell shakedown. They had hoped to gain enough evidence to nail not only Danny but also his associates working on the outside and, hopefully, any prison officers who might be on the take from Danny's activities. As it was, they had to cut their losses, believing that at least they had enough evidence to get a conviction against Danny Faries. After the cell raid they confronted Danny.

'He said: 'No problem', an officer recalled later. 'He'd show us how he did everything. He said the guards were bringing him lobster dinners and allowing him to get laid during visits.'

Metro-Dade Police handed over all their statements and evidence to the Florida State Attorney's office and waited for fraud charges to be brought against Danny. But nothing happened.

At first they were told that charges would have to wait, pending the outcome of Danny's murder trial. Then, months later, the case against the Jailhouse Shopping Company was suddenly dropped.

No official reason was given. But Larry LaVecchio, chief of the state attorney's Organised Crime Division, who had all the evidence firmly in his lap at the time, was reported as saying: 'There is very little deterrent value in bringing a couple of minor felonies to court when a guy is facing the electric chair.' LaVecchio said the evidence of corruption among Danny's guards was not strong enough to gain a conviction, and would rely almost solely on Danny's uncorroborated statements.

This caused a huge row between police investigators and the state attorney's office. Finally, in April 1989, Assistant State Attorney Gary Bagleibter wrote an official memo closing the case once and for all. It said that using the evidence of an accused murderer against prison guards could not lead to a successful prosecution.

The memo even criticised Metro-Dade Police for getting Danny to cooperate over the corruption allegations, which it called 'cases of minimal import'. As one angry police officer commented wryly: 'I wonder, how can corruption in the Dade County Jail be of minimal import?'

Investigator Raul Ubieta, whose plea to have the phone removed from Danny's cell was rejected, later recalled diplomatically: 'Any time an inquiry doesn't come to a proper conclusion it's frustration for us'. His partner Ross Hughes said: 'This guy was already in jail for murder – possibly facing the electric chair – so he had no fear of any reprisal for the fraud he was committing. He was very comfortable in that role'.

While all this wrangling was going on, Danny Faries was moved from cell 10 B3 to cell 104 in the nearby Interim Central Detention Centre. Incredibly, he still had access to a telephone. No-one knew why.

Shocked police investigators demanded a meeting with the Department of Corrections to find out what was going on. They reported in a memo later that the corrections officers felt 'there was no legal basis for imposing prohibitions or restrictions on inmates' access to a telephone'.

Danny Faries was still in business. In fact, he was delighted with his new office.

He had cell 104 to himself and shared the phone with only five other inmates in other cells. He said later: 'About the only difference the move made was to give me some more privacy. I didn't have so many people looking over my shoulder all the time'.

Danny's only problem was that his store of credit card numbers was drying up. It is possible that his team of crooked sales assistants on the outside had heard about the police investigation and had decided to resign from the Jailhouse Shopping Company. Frustrated, Danny spent weeks thinking of a new corporate strategy. And then it hit him – a plan so simple that he was surprised he hadn't thought of it before then.

Danny took out an advertisement in America's only national newspaper, *USA Today,* for a company called Regina Donovan Cosmetics. It advertised $90-worth of top quality women's cosmetics for the bargain price of $19.95. All credit cards accepted. Danny hired an answering service in New York for a week and the calls flooded in. There were no cosmetics, of course, but the callers dutifully left their names, addresses, card numbers, expiry dates…all the information that Danny needed.

'It was like a gold mine', Danny was reported as saying later. Business boomed. Danny was delighted.

In a characteristic fit of 'generosity', he even ordered an expensive set of weights and work-out equipment for the detention centre gym...on a stolen credit card number, naturally.

Danny later revealed to viewers of the American TV show *Sixty Minutes* exactly how he had managed to keep his business going despite the seizure by jail officials of hundreds of credit card numbers from his cell. He said that after the raid he still had one hidden card number 'written on the bottom of my bunk. It was a woman's card. Regina Donovan was the name. It was a good number and I said, well here we go – we gotta do something!'

So Faries set up the phony phone-order company, with girls working for him answering calls from customers ordering non-existent Regina Donovan cosmetics on credit. Danny went on:

'The girls took the orders, saying "Thank you for calling Regina Donovan, may we help you and what credit card will we be using today?" They wrote down the number and the expiry date, and at the end of the day I'd call them and they'd have this whole new stack of numbers. It was incredible!'

By early 1989 Danny had managed to postpone his murder trial date several times simply by firing one defence lawyer after another. Around this time, however, a telephone company called TELCO noticed that the number of long-distance calls made on fraudulent credit card numbers had increased in Southern Florida by a staggering 4,000 per cent. Painstakingly, the company went through the figures and were surprised to discover that no fewer than 1,500 of these calls could be traced to the telephone outside cell 104 of the Interim Central Detention Centre in Dade County.

TELCO by-passed both the police and the Corrections Department and called in the US Secret Service. The Jailhouse Shopping Company was about to go into liquidation.

It took 10 months for federal agents to get the evidence on Danny Faries. During that time they established documentary proof that he had stolen $750,000. But they were convinced that the real figure was nearer $4 million. They raided Danny's cell twice and found thousands of credit card numbers. One senior agent asked the Department of Corrections why, in the light of the previous police investigation, Danny was still allowed near a phone. He was told that there was an administrative rule that 'this particular class of prisoner in this particular cell block was entitled to access to a telephone'. Rules were made not to be broken.

Danny was locked in his cell 24 hours a day while the Secret Service prepared their case against him. During that time he was allowed to use the phone for only 15 minutes, and then under the strictest supervision. Nevertheless, Danny claimed that business went on as usual.

He boasted that he had managed to run a telephone wire into his cell from the nursing office next door. Someone smuggled him in a telephone and he rigged the whole thing up to his cell light so that, instead of ringing, the light flashed and the guards were not alerted.

Even Danny Faries could postpone his murder trial no longer. On 16 May, four years after the crime, he was convicted of the first-degree murder of his partying pal and was sentenced to 25 years.

Federal agents hauled him off to the Metropolitan Correctional Centre in Chicago to await trial on fraud charges. Danny refused a defence lawyer and decided to represent himself. This gave him access to all the prosecution evidence against him.

Among this weighty file, Danny found a credit card statement belonging to a Mr Fletcher Waller of Washington State. It appeared that the unfortunate Mr Waller's account had been debited for $3,000 of computer equipment about which he knew nothing. Danny took careful note of this piece of evidence.

In court, Danny pleaded guilty to one charge of fraud and was given a further five years. He was ordered to serve his time in a federal prison, not the most hospitable climate in which to spend 30 years of one's life, as Danny knew well. At the prison reception centre Danny suddenly complained of paranoiac visions that a fearsome vengeful figure was trying to hunt him down…and went conveniently cuckoo.

He was promptly dispatched to Charlotte Correctional Institution near peaceful Fort Myers, on Florida's west coast. There, in the much higher-security state 'psychiatric facility', he claimed to have put the credit card business behind him. Cynics were not so sure.

Pete Collins is the man who knows more about Daniel Faries than perhaps anyone else. A teacher at Jackson High School who became fascinated by the Faries case, he met Danny and began collating material for a book on the amiable con man.

In 1991 the row over lack of action taken to curb Danny's excesses became the subject of an investigation in the *Miami Herald*, principally due to the thorough researches of Collins, who was by now a freelance writer based in Miami. He told a television audience:

'When I was interviewing him you could call him up at any time of the day or night and he would be working around the clock. He was operating in as many as 40 states. There were as many as 150 drop sites, dozens of employees, $750,000 documented in stolen goods – perhaps in reality up to two to four million dollars – and that was just during an eleven-month window of his captivity.'

The row will rumble on for years over how Danny Faries managed to operate his bizarre one-man crime wave. How did he get away with it for so long? As Danny himself said: 'Even on the outside of my cell door I had Master Card and Visa logos. It was pretty wide open.'

Asked how the Faries scam could have continued for so many years, the man in charge, Lonnie Lawrence, Director of Dade County Corrections, commented: 'We don't have a perfect system.'

THERESE HUMBERT

Mademoiselle Thérèse was no beauty. The provincial washerwoman was as podgy as she was penniless. Yet the French peasant girl had a certain magnetism that won over the rich and famous – and won her the hand in marriage of a trusting husband. Her charismatic attraction also made her a fortune.

Thérèse was the daughter of Gilbert Aurignac, a peasant farmer from the little town of Beauzelle, near Toulouse. Gilbert neglected his fields to spend idle days in cafes drinking himself into a stupor on cheap red wine. He would regale his fellow drinkers with unlikely tales of his family's former glory, of how his real name was d'Aurignac and how he had been disowned by his aristocratic father. His children, however, would inherit vast wealth upon his death.

Gilbert Aurignac's children were Thérèse, the oldest, born in 1860, two brothers and a young sister. They too had heard their father's boastful story, so often that they believed it. When he died in 1874 they learned the truth: they were left paupers.

Thérèse, however, had learned one other truth ...that the world is full of gullible people who will believe anything if it is repeated often enough.

To help keep her family fed, Thérèse first took in washing, and then went to work as a laundry maid at the home of the mayor of Toulouse, an ambitious lawyer and politician named Gustave Humbert. There she allowed herself to be seduced by her boss' son, Frédéric, to whom she wove a most astonishing story.

As a youngster, she said, she had attracted the attention of a rich spinster named Mademoiselle de Marcotte. Now very old and without any surviving relatives, this venerable lady had written a will bequeathing her entire estate, including its château and vineyards, to Thérèse. Frédéric believed every word of her tale, fell madly in love with her and, despite his father's protestations, secretly married her.

Frédéric took Thérèse to Paris, where he launched a career as an advocate. The fees he earned, however, were wholly insufficient to sustain the extraordinary spending of his ex-washerwoman wife. She fell in love with 'Gay Paree' and entered into the social whirl. On the back of her 'inheritance' the couple borrowed more and more money – until one day their creditors checked on her benefactor's identity and found there was no such person as Mademoiselle de Marcotte.

There were several things that Thérèse could have done. She could have fled the city. She could have stuck to her story. She could have owned up to her fraud. Or she could simply pile fresh lies upon the old ones. Thérèse chose the latter course.

Her story about Mademoiselle de Marcotte had indeed been untrue, she said. But she had fabricated the tale only to disguise the true identity of her benefactor. He was one Robert Henry Crawford, a millionaire from Chicago, whom she had met on a train two years previously. They had become firm friends and when he subsequently suffered a heart attack, she had nursed him back to health. Mr Crawford had since died, however, and had left his fortune to be shared between his two nephews in the United States and Thérèse's younger sister Marie. Marie, then still a schoolgirl, would not receive her inheritance until she was 21 years of age...but in the meantime Thérèse was to receive an annual income of just under $100,000.

One of the people to whom Thérèse told this fresh pack of lies was her father-in-law, Gustave Humbert. The Toulouse mayor had risen rapidly in the world of politics and was now Minister of Justice in the national government. Whether or not he believed Thérèse's tale, she nevertheless persuaded him to pay all her and Frédéric's Paris creditors to avoid a family scandal. In turn, she 'repaid' old Monsieur Humbert by announcing that the documents containing her inheritance had been placed by American lawyers in a locked safe, the administration and secure keeping of which had been guaranteed by the Humbert family until her sister Marie came of age.

As Paris buzzed with the story of the 'Crawford Inheritance', Thérèse boldly turned up at the bank to which she had previously owed the most money. Warmly welcomed by the manager, she told him: 'Sadly, Monsieur, I am not permitted to open the safe and exercise the bonds and securities therein until Marie comes of age. Otherwise, I am in danger of forfeiting all claim upon the Crawford millions'.

Predictably, she then asked for a loan. It was readily given. Thérèse repeated the trick at banks throughout Paris – and elsewhere. One Toulouse bank alone advanced her seven million francs. Much of the money was used to purchase a lavish mansion in the capital, in her bedroom of which she installed a safe supposedly containing the secrets of the fortune belonging to her and her little sister.

The door of this massive, fireproof steel structure was opened only once – when she invited an over-awed provincial notary to examine a number of bundles of paper and to itemise the wrappers that supposedly indicated their contents. Then the safe was locked and thick wax seals were applied to the doors and handles. The imposing safe was not to be opened again until Marie's 21st birthday.

Meanwhile, Thérèse and Frédèric embarked on a spending spree of unprecedented proportions. Thérèse also invited sister Marie and their two brothers, Emile and Romain, to join her in an orgy of extravagance.

The human cash dispenser became known in Paris society as 'La Grande Thérèse' as the ample-bosomed lady swept in and out of restaurants and fashion salons and opera boxes.

Only one mishap threatened their idyll. A Lyon banker named Delatte visited Thérèse at her Paris mansion to arrange the advance of a further loan secured on the inheritance. Idly, he inquired where in the United States her late benefactor had lived. Off the top of her head, Thérèse replied: 'Somerville, a suburb of Boston.'

Unbeknown to Thérèse, the Lyon banker was about to sail to the States and, while in Boston, made enquiries about the fictitious millionaire James Henry Crawford. Realising that no-one had ever heard of such a person, Monsieur Delatte wrote to a fellow banker in France telling him of his suspicions. But before further investigations could be made in the United States, Delatte mysteriously vanished. After a few days his body was fished out of the East River, New York. He had been murdered.

The killer was never uncovered. But it has always been assumed that Delatte's untimely death was what would now be known as a 'contract killing', ordered by Thérèse or her brothers. After he had been taken care of, it took only the glib tongue of 'La Grande Thérèse' to calm the fears of the French banker to whom Delatte had written.

The threat of exposure evaporated, as did the cash that the Humbert clan continued to borrow, which had now reached an estimated 65 million francs!

There was one event that Thérèse Humbert could not influence, however...the 21st birthday of sister Marie. The day was looming like a time bomb ticking away inside the great safe.

Thérèse countered with two plans. The first was to distract attention from the vital birthday by inventing a dispute between herself and the non-existent nephews from the States, over where the securities should be stored. Her second ploy was for her brothers to establish a finance house in a rented building in fashionable Boulevard des Capucines and to seek investment business through a chain of salesmen. Early investors found their returns swift and satisfactorily high, and the money flowed in. None of it was invested, of course. Apart from the small sums paid out in high 'interest', the rest was put aside to repay some of the more pressing creditors who wanted their loans repaid the moment Marie came of age.

The whole corrupt edifice began to collapse, however, when a Bank of France official, Jules Bizat, investigated the invested funds of the Humbert brothers' finance house and found that there were none. He went straight to the Prime Minister, Pierre Marie Waldeck-Rousseau. Fearing that official any involvement would have the effect of precipitating yet another governmental scandal (there had already been several at the close of the 19th century) the premier decided to leak the story to the Paris newspaper *Le Matin*. Thérèse had no alternative but to protest her innocence while fending off the relentless demands of her creditors.

Now began an extraordinary chain of events. The Humberts' lawyer, Maître du Buit, believed so fervently in the truth of the Crawford Inheritance that he threatened to sue the newspaper for libel and offered to open the safe to clear her name. This was the very last thing that Thérèse wanted, of course, and she panicked. On 8 May 1902, two days before the safe was due to be opened by du Buit, Thérèse or one of her accomplices set fire to the upper floor of her home. Her bedroom was gutted, destroying everything apart from the safe, which proved itself to be totally fireproof.

Thérèse, now enmeshed in a web of her own lies, assembled her sister, her brothers and husband Frédéric, and took a train to an unknown destination. So she was nowhere to be found when, on the appointed day, lawyer du Buit led an anxious band of businessmen and bankers into Thérèse's bedroom. The wax seals were broken, the doors were unlocked and eager hands swung them back to reveal…a single house brick!

Many years ago, upon the death of Thérèse's boastful father, Gilbert Aurignac, his children had stood around as Madame Aurignac turned the key in an old oak chest which, he had long boasted, contained papers documenting the family's secret fortune. It too had contained nothing but a brick. Now Thérèse was repeating history, though for a much more august company.

The aftermath of the discovery in Thérèse's bedroom safe in 1902 reverberated around the social and financial circles of France. Ten suicides were attributed to her fraudulent machinations, one of them that of a leading banker.

Of the lady herself, there was no sign. She and her family remained undetected for seven months until Spanish police traced them to a Madrid lodging house. They were extradited and, in February 1903, the arch tricksters – Thérèse, Frédéric, Emile and Romain – were sent for trial on no fewer than 257 charges of forgery and fraud. On 8 August they stood in the dock at the Palais de Justice, while queues formed outside the court comprised of thousands of spectators from all over France. Special trains had even been laid on, such was the fascination for this 'trial of the century'. They were disappointed to see a plump, sallow old woman whose once-magnetic personality had deserted her. A foreign newsman disparagingly called her 'a typical French cook'.

Thérèse and Frédéric were each sentenced to five years in prison. Romain got three years and Emile two. 'La Grande Thérèse' was released after three-and-a-half years because of her good conduct in jail. She hid herself away in the countryside and died – largely forgotten – during World War I, in 1917.

And what became of the brick? – The piece of clay and the charred metal safe surrounding it went on display in a Paris shop window, where it became something of a tourist attraction.

ANTHONY WILLIAMS

Had the criminal whom fraud squad detectives succeeded in tracking down been anyone else, London's Metropolitan Police would have heartily welcomed the attention. But as it was, they could only bury their heads in their hands in shocked disbelief.

The villain they had nabbed for filtering away funds meant for undercover operations was one of their own. And Scotland Yard's deputy director of finance, Anthony Williams, could only put his hands up to the crime, relieved that nearly 12 years of lies, deception and downright theft were finally over. There was also the small question of a missing £5 million, used to finance Williams' secret life – a life which had him opening bank accounts around the world, living as a nobleman, 'owning' virtually an entire village in Scotland and recognised as a man of considerable substance and property just about everywhere else.

There may have been some who admired one of the 20th century's cheekiest con men. But others, like Sir Paul Condon, the Metropolitan Police Commissioner, were left to pick up the pieces of their biggest, most humiliating inside job ever.

Appearances can be deceptive – mild-mannered
accountant Anthony Williams' outrageous deceit led
to public humiliation for the Metropolitan Police.

At a press conference, Sir Paul offered the people of London an 'unreserved apology', admitting he was 'angry and embarrassed that the courageous work of police officers had been betrayed'. There was only one thing he could confidently reassure everyone of: that such a crime would never happen again.

It was an incredible and intriguing trail of corruption that led to the police apology and to 55-year-old Williams' sentence of seven-and-a-half years' imprisonment on 19 May 1995.

The astonishing catalogue of deceit had begun with one small theft in 1981. The sum was £200. Officially, the cash was earmarked as payment for an officer to take his seriously-ill wife on holiday. But the excuse was fictitious and in reality the £200 was pocketed by Williams.

Having succeeded so easily in his first attempt at crime, the mild-mannered accountant stole again and again – and kept on stealing right under the noses of Britain's nucleus of top crime-busters. He was in a convenient position to make stealing easy, for he was overseer of the Met's staff welfare fund, from which he began to make regular 'withdrawals'.

Just once, Williams got close to being caught. A colleague noticed that one sum didn't quite add up. Williams quickly paid in a cheque to cover the discrepancy. In total, the bespectacled, respected handler of police welfare funds siphoned off £7000.

This money which should have gone to the hard-up and the ill. A lot of the loot was used to ease Williams' own money problems, caused by the end of his first marriage. He had a commitment of £500 monthly maintenance payments for his two daughters. The welfare fund also came in handy to clear an overdraft.

Over the years, Williams grew proud of his deception. His bravado as an accountant who could not only cook the books but make them boil, grew. Without really knowing where he could get his hands on unlimited money, Williams opened an account at Coutts, bankers to the Queen and to the upper-crust. Williams' creation of an 'uncle in Norway' who was set to leave him a healthy inheritance not only smoothed the way with Coutts (the bank authorised a £30,000 overdraft) but was later to prove invaluable when questions were raised about his high-living ways.

In 1986, Williams was to strike gold. As deputy finance director, Scotland Yard could find no-one better to handle police affairs of a highly confidential and sensitive nature. Williams was been put in charge of a 'secret fund' to fight organised crime. There was speculation that this fund was used to pay police informers and for general undercover work – but, if true, only a proportion of the fund was allocated for this purpose.

In fact, for over eight years Williams administered two companies operating an anti-terrorist surveillance aircraft based at a Surrey airfield. Throughout the period when he was financing the running of the plane, IRA mainland bombing was at its peak and police needed an aircraft to keep watch on suspected arms caches and 'safe houses'. So secret was the project that just a handful of people within Scotland Yard knew of the operation and of Williams' involvement in it. So hush-hush was the project that any curious outsiders would find the tracks totally covered. All that seemed to be in existence were two firms, one apparently owned by the other, running a small, fixed-wing aeroplane.

Such was the determination by anti-terrorist squads to control the IRA's activities that the Cessna plane was in constant use. For instance, in 1989 it was used in a successful operation leading to the capture of two IRA activists, Damien Comb and Liam O'Dhuibhir, at an arms dump on a desolate beach on the Pembrokeshire coast of South Wales. They were caught after a seven-week stake-out, codenamed Operation Pebble. It greatly suited Williams' purposes that the plane was so heavily used. Such victories against IRA terrorists meant few worries were raised over the Cessna's costs – which amounted to £250,000 in the first year alone – allowing Williams to rob the fund blind.

Whatever the Cessna operation required, Williams would immediately pay. The money was swiftly provided. No complaints were made about his speedy requisitioning of anything from aviation fuel to paperclips. What was to come to light when Williams eventually stood trial, however, was that over eight years he requisitioned £7 million – with only around £2 million actually being spent!

The Old Bailey court was told: 'The defendant was allowed unlimited private access on his own discretion to the funds of the Receiver (Scotland Yard's financial controller). It was placed in a specified account. He did not have to answer to anyone...he controlled the payments in and the payments out.'

As the money rolled in, Williams was glad that he had his 'uncle' in Norway to explain away such untold, unquestioned wealth. The inheritance story fended off enquiries about his grand homes and grand lifestyle. And Williams certainly knew how to splash the cash around!

The money was spread across banks and building societies in Scotland, London and the Channel Islands. Sometimes Williams even paid cash for one of the many properties he acquired. Payment for an apartment was made directly from the secret Scotland Yard fund. In 1989 alone, Williams stole more than £1 million.

It was remarkable that Williams' wife Kay happily accepted the 'Norwegian uncle' story to explain the couple's elevation into a style of living most only dream of. It was even more remarkable that no-one at Scotland Yard got wind of the millionaire lifestyle of Williams, whose salary was £42,000 a year.

He brought homes in Leatherhead and Haslemere in Surrey and a flat in London's Westminster. He rented another flat in Mayfair which cost him £2000 a month. Friends he entertained there lavishly marvelled at Williams' good fortune in having a foreign relative who had left him such wealth. Yet another house in New Malden, Surrey, was purchased for £178,000 cash. A holiday villa on Spain's Costa del Sol was added to the property empire.

As well as Coutts, where he was given a gold bank card, Williams opened accounts at National Westminster, Standard Chartered and Clydesdale banks, plus Bradford & Bingley and the Leeds Building Societies. But it was in Scotland where Williams' stolen wealth allowed him to feel as if he owned the world.

Williams had fallen in love with the Highlands village of Tomintoul where he had spent several happy visits. So in 1989 he decided to buy a large chunk of it. First there was a £6000 cottage in The Square, on which Williams carried out £400,000 renovations. Then there was the £120,000 Gordon

Arms Hotel, which underwent £1.5 million restoration, the old fire station (£21,000) and the Manse in Glenlivet (£192,000). Williams even had the cheek to apply for a Business Expansion Scheme grant for one of his companies, Tomintoul Enterprises, from the Moray Enterprise Board. Tomintoul Enterprises provided £3 million towards Williams's regeneration of the little village.

The good people of Tomintoul hailed Williams as a saviour. And indeed, to them, he was. He created hundreds of jobs at his hotel, pub and restaurant – at one time the hotel employed seven chefs – and sponsored local events including the Tomintoul Highland Games. The villagers had even more reason to believe the Lord had provided. For Williams invested £70,000 on acquiring the title Laird before taking over Tomintoul. Not content with one feudal title, Williams bought himself another eight at a cost of £144,000.

When their Laird of Tomintoul was finally arrested, the villagers could only speak well of him. 'I know what he did was wrong, but it wasn't that bad', remarked George McAllister, 60, in charge of the local museum. 'Most of these fraud types spirit the money away into foreign bank accounts or investments abroad. But he didn't. He put most of it back here, into our wee place. It really made Tomintoul a better place. Just look around you.'

Iain Birnie, running the village shop, said: 'So it was money from London? Big deal. They've got enough of the stuff down there anyway. It should be coming north. Tony Williams did a damn sight more good with it up here than it would ever have done down south.'

Williams' eventual downfall came when banks grew suspicious about the large and endless amounts of cash he was depositing. It was believed something more sinister than downright fraud was afoot. So, as obliged to in such cases under the Drugs Trafficking Offences Act, they disclosed their worries to the police. Williams' arrest came in July 1994. Two months later he was dismissed from his job.

At his trial, Williams pleaded guilty to 17 charges of theft from the Receiver of Scotland Yard and two charges of theft from the civilian staff's welfare fund. Williams initially denied any charges relating to the welfare fund – simply, said his barrister James Sturman, because he had completely forgotten about the crime.

Williams asked for 535 other charges to be taken into consideration. In all, he had stolen £5,320,737 of the £7,413,761 entrusted to him over the years.

Mr Sturman told the court that it had been a relief when Williams was finally caught. Apart from a few panic-struck lies and half-truths when first arrested, Williams had fully cooperated with the police.

Around £529,000 of the stolen funds had been recovered and there were hopes of a further £200,000 to £300,000, the court heard.

Mr Sturman added that Williams felt terrible remorse for his sins and had expressed as much to priests. 'He has lied to his wife, he has lied to his friends, he has lived a lie', said Mr Sturman.

Referring to Williams' double life in Scotland, prosecuting counsel Brian Barker QC summed up Williams' influence on the Highland village he had changed out of all recognition. He said: 'The suburban civil servant became, when he crossed the border, a nobleman and benefactor of Tomintoul.'

Williams did not call any character witnesses. The defendant told the court: 'I don't want to put my good friends in the box to say I was honest. Obviously, I haven't been for years.'

Sentencing Williams to six and a half years in prison for thefts from his employers and one year for stealing from the welfare fund, the Recorder, Sir Lawrence Verney, told him: 'Such crimes are inexcusable. No-one minded to follow your example must be left in any doubt as to the consequences.'

Williams, still bearing a healthy tan from his travels, left the dock to begin his sentence, clutching the carrier bag which contained what seemed now his only worldly goods. His 47-year-old wife vowed to stand by him.

Two investigations were launched into just how Williams got away with his criminal activities for so long, one concentrating on the civil welfare fund, the other on the secret fund.

The folk of Tomintoul were left scratching their heads – and left to pick up the pieces of a property explosion which no longer had funds available to sustain it. They knew many jobs would have to go. They knew there could come a time when feet stopped walking over the £25,000 carpet in the Gordon Hotel's public bar.

There was just one last reminder of 'Lord' Williams – a new brand of ale cheekily labelled 'Laird of Tomintoul Beer' and bearing a label of a Metropolitan Police helmet.

ROBIN HOOD

His is a name that has, against all the odds, survived for six centuries. His fame is as a criminal, a violent outlaw and highway robber who, with a band of common thieves, plundered the traffic of the king's highway. Yet he is the most enduring hero of his age. He is Robin Hood.

Details about this legendary outlaw, who dwelt in Sherwood Forest in the late 13th or early 14th century, have always been scant. His reprehensible activities were seemingly minor, and he was not immortalised in any great literature. It was the illiterate peasantry of the Middle Ages who passed on his name, his fame and his supposed deeds by word of mouth from one generation to another, in ballads and fireside stories. As a result, an obscure criminal with no place in history acquired international fame.

There can be few people who have not now heard of Robin Hood, through books, movies and television series. Most of the modern-day images, however, owe more to scriptwriters' imagination than to historical research. The romanticism of the character has not helped the cause of the outlaw's reputation against the attacks of the cynics.

Historians over the centuries have debated the issue, challenging his adventures and disagreeing on the dashing vagabond's true identity. James Holt, professor of medieval history at Cambridge University, and author of a book on the outlaw, says: 'Robin Hood was nothing like he was portrayed. He wore a hood, like a monk's cowl. But there is absolutely no evidence that he robbed the rich and gave to the poor. That was added to the legend 200 years or more after his death'.

Cynics have also pointed to the fact that Robin's supposed rule of the English 'badlands' was only briefly reported within the 200 years following his death. He was fleetingly referred to by the Scottish historian Fordun, who died in 1386, but following this there was no further written word of his exploits until the 16th century.

Then, however, chronicler John Stow paid him high tribute. According to Stow, Robin Hood's band had a complement of 100 men, all tall and good archers. They were fed and clothed by the spoils he took, yet he 'suffered no woman to be oppressed or otherwise molested. Poor men's goods he spared, abuntantlie relieving them with which by theft he got from abbeys and houses of rich earles'.

So how much of the Robin Hood legend is true?

Records show that in the 13th and 14th centuries there lived in Wakefield, Yorkshire, a real Robin Hood who may have been the legendary outlaw. This Robin, christened Robert Hood, was born in about

Folklore hero Robin Hood has taken on many guises throughout the centuries – here he is depicted in philanthropic and uncharacteristically humble mode, bearing a friar across a river.

1290. His father, Adam Hood, was a forester in the service of John Earl Warenne, lord of the manor of Wakefield. The surname in old court documents is variously spelt Hod, Hode and Hood.

On 25 January 1316 Robin Hood's 'handmaid' is recorded as having been brought before a court for taking dry wood and 'vert' from the 'old oak'. Vert is the old English term for trees which provide shelter and food for deer. She was fined two pence. Other court records for the year 1316 show that Robin Hood and his wife Matilda paid two shillings 'for leave to take one piece of land of the lord's waste' to build a five-roomed house.

In 1322, Robin's landlord – at this time, Thomas, Earl of Lancaster – called his tenants to arms in rebellion against King Edward II. A tenant had no choice but to obey his lord implicitly, and Robin Hood followed the earl into battle as an archer. The revolt was crushed, Lancaster was tried for treason and beheaded. His estates were forfeited to the king and his followers were outlawed.

Robin Hood fled into Barnsdale Forest, which at that time covered about 80 sq km/30 sq miles of Yorkshire and was linked to Nottinghamshire's Sherwood Forest, with an area of about 65 sq km/25 sq miles. The forests were traversed by the Roman-built Great North Road, with its rich pickings for robbers. And so the legend of Robin Hood was born.

One of Robin's supposed escapades along this highway concerns the haughty bishop of Hereford, who was travelling to York when he came across the outlaw leader and some of his companions roasting venison. Taking them for peasants, and infuriated by this flagrant breach of forest laws, the bishop demanded an explanation. The outlaws calmly told him that they were about to dine. The bishop ordered his attendants to seize them.

The outlaws begged for mercy but the bishop swore that he would show them none. So Robin blew on his horn, and the unhappy bishop found himself surrounded by archers in Lincoln green. They took him prisoner, with all his company, and demanded a ransom, amusing themselves by making him dance a jig around a large oak tree. The tree is no longer there but the ground on which it stood is known as Bishop's Tree Root.

Several other oak trees in Barnsdale and Sherwood are associated with Robin Hood and his band. Centre Tree, half way between Thoresby and Wellbeck, is said to be the marker from which Robin Hood's network of secret routes stretched through the forest.

The most famous tree, however, is Major Oak, at Birkland. It is reputedly a thousand years old and has a girth of about 29 feet. Alfred, Lord Tennyson visited this oak in the 19th century and in his poem

The Foresters, has Little John referring to it as '...that oak where twelve men can stand inside nor touch each other'.

Among the stories passed down the centuries about Robin's prowess is that of a visit he made with his closest friend, Little John, to Whitby Abbey. The abbot asked them to demonstrate their skill with the bow by shooting from the monastery roof. Both did so, and the arrows fell either side of a lane at Whitby Lathes, more than a mile away. The abbot had two stone pillars erected on the spots where the arrows fell, which survived until the end of the 18th century. The fields on either side were also named after the event: Robin Hood's Close and Little John's Close.

Little John, who was Robin's second-in-command, was not a merry man, as often portrayed, but a rather miserable and touchy fellow. He got his nickname because of a jest about his height. He was said to have died at Hathersage, in Derbyshire, and his grave there was reopened in 1784. In it were found the bones of an exceptionally tall man.

Professor Holt says of Robin's right-hand man that he was capable of brutal murder. 'He slew a monk suspected of betraying his master. Then he cut off the head of the monk's young servant so that there would be no witnesses.'

Another principal member of Robin's band was Friar Tuck, possibly a composite character of two fat friars, one of whom enjoyed good food and drink, the other a lover of morris dancing. Alternatively, he may have been Robert Stafford, an early 15th century chaplain of Lindfield, in Sussex, who used the alias Friar Tuck after a royal warrant was issued for his arrest in 1417 on charges of robbery and murder.

Professor Holt explains: 'Friar Tuck is, according to legend, a jolly fellow who ate huge meals, amused the outlaws and fought with a wooden staff. Yet records show that the original Friar Tuck organised a second outlaw band 200 miles away – and hundreds of years after Robin Hood was active. There was nothing jolly about him; it seems he burned and pillaged the homes of his enemies.'

As for Robin's supposed lover Maid Marian, latest research shows she was the product of a 13th century poem, written a generation after Robin's death, and therefore sadly never kissed her sweetheart in the leafy glades of Sherwood Forest. 'In the poem', says Professor Holt, 'she had to defend her virtue against a knight for the sake of preserving her chastity for her lover, who just happened to be called Robin. She was adopted into the Robin Hood legend 200 years later.'

But whoever comprised Robin's outlaw band, they certainly got around the country. Robin Hood's Bay, away on the Yorkshire coast, was named after him. It was here that the outlaws were reputed to own several boats, which they kept for fishing and for possible escape from the authorities.

On one of his journeys, Robin Hood visited St Mary's Church, Nottingham, where a monk in the congregation recognised him and alerted the sheriff. Robin drew his sword and slew 12 soldiers before being captured. But before he could be brought to trial, Little John led a band of the outlaws into Nottingham and rescued him. They also sought out the monk who had originally reported their leader to the sheriff – and, as historian Holt points out, murdered him.

But it was Robin Hood's supposed championing of the underdog that made him into a folk hero. His robbing of the rich and gifts to the poor, and his flouting of unpopular authority, became an inspiration to the oppressed peasantry of old England.

On one famous occasion, Robin Hood was supposed to have met King Edward II. The story goes that the king, hearing that the herds of royal deer in Sherwood were diminishing because of the appetites of Robin Hood and his band, determined to get rid of the outlaws. So he and his knights disguised themselves as monks and rode into the forest. They were met by Robin Hood and some of his band, who demanded money.

The king gave them £40, saying that was all he had. Robin took £20 for his men and gave the rest back to the king. Edward then produced the royal seal and told the outlaw leader that the king wished to see him in Nottingham. Robin summoned all his men to kneel before the seal and swear their love for the king. They then invited the 'monks' to eat with them – and fed them on the king's venison. Later Edward revealed his identity and pardoned all the outlaws, on condition that they would come to his court and serve him.

The story is told in *A Lytell Geste of Robin Hood*, published in 1459. It may not be complete fiction; the king was certainly in Nottingham in November 1323, and the story of his action is in keeping with what is known of his character.

A few months later, in 1324, the name of Robin Hood appears in the household accounts of Edward II. There is a record of wages paid to him until November of the same year. After that date, he vanishes into folklore again. Perhaps after enjoying the free life of an outlaw, he was unable to settle in service, even for his king.

Robin Hood's adventures in the forests continued until about 1346 when he is reputed to have died at Kirklees Priory. The prioress there, said to be his cousin Elizabeth de Stainton, is reputed to have hastened his death. When he begged her to help relieve his pain during an illness, she bled him until he was too weak to recover.

On his death-bed, so the story concluded, Robin Hood managed to blow his famous hunting-horn, which summoned his faithful companion Little John to his side. Robin then shot an arrow from the window of his room and asked to be buried wherever it might fall.

Richard Grafton, who wrote a story about the outlaw band in 1569, said that a tomb was set up at that point by the prioress. But the reason is not flattering to the Robin Hood of popular legend. Grafton wrote:

'The prioresse of the same place caused him to be buried by the highway side, where he had used to rob and spoyle those that passed that way. And upon his grave the sayde prioresse did lay a very fayre stone wherein his name was graven. And the cause why she buried him there was that for the common strangers and travellers, knowyng and seeyng him there buryed, might more safely and without feare take their journeys that was, which they durst not do in the life of the sayd outlawes. And at either end of the sayde tombe was erected a crosse of stone, which is to be seen there at present.'

The stone is no longer there, but the spot claimed to be the grave of Robin Hood can still be seen to this very day.

BERNIE CORNFELD

When a small, tubby, wrinkled ex-jailbird called Bernie Cornfeld died in March 1995, all the newspaper photographs accompanying his obituary showed him with a beaming smile – and usually surrounded by beautiful young women. How did the old crook lead such a happy life?

On the face of it, Bernie Cornfeld had little to smile about. He had perpetrated one of the most extraordinarily audacious frauds in history, had been uncovered, disgraced, severely censured and locked up in prison.

He had once owned a private jet, a Beverly Hills mansion, a house in Belgravia, London, and châteaux in France and Switzerland – all bought with other people's money. He had never seemed to care a damn about those he defrauded, although he must have felt the loss when the courts removed most of his wealth.

Nor was he very gallant about the women in his life. He once said: 'A beautiful woman with a brain is like a beautiful woman with a club foot.'

Yet until his dying day, at the age of 67, Bernie Cornfeld shared his Californian home with eight beautiful women, with two more waiting for his call in London.

What was the secret that kept the selfish old fraud smiling to the very end?

Bernie Cornfeld was a former schoolteacher in the United States who became one of the smoothest, brightest and most successful salesmen the world has ever known.

As head of his own company, Investors Overseas Services (IOS), which he founded in Switzerland in 1965, he recruited an army of salespeople by promising them untold riches. As an incentive, he would invite them to his palace on Lake Geneva, his French chateau or his Beverly Hills mansion, where they could witness the trappings of the fabulous wealth that could also be theirs.

Cornfeld also liked to show off his harem of 20 or so beautiful girlfriends who lived in his exotic homes and to display his stables of racehorses and expensive cars. He boasted of his romantic friendships with international glamour girls.

The message to his staff was clear. Few could resist the blunt question he always asked them and for which he became famous: 'Do you sincerely want to be rich?'

As far as 10,000 salespeople and 100,000 investors in 95 countries were concerned, the answer had to be a resounding 'Yes'. As punters rushed to part with their savings, IOS grew into a mammoth insurance and investment fund which controlled more

Former schoolteacher Bernie Cornfeld attained a life of riches not only through his magnetic personality, but also through unashamed exploitation.

than £1 billion in stocks and shares. Within five years the assets of IOS were spread among investments which included oil prospecting, electronics, insurance and gold fields. Some of these were profitable, but others lost money.

Many of the sales force did indeed become wealthy, earning colossal fees in commissions for enrolling more subscribers. But most of the unfortunate investors made little or nothing – and many lost the lot as their funds were squandered to sustain the unashamed luxury of the wild–spending IOS boss. Cornfeld's personal stake in the company grew to £100 million.

The bubble had to burst, of course. IOS needed top expand at an impossible rate to keep paying its sales commissions, quite apart from the boss's perks. Indeed, Cornfeld's publicly excessive lifestyle scandalised the conservative Swiss financial authorities and they announced that they were investigating his entire set-up.

There were worries that IOS assets were being mismanaged, and that much of its wealth existed only on paper.

By 1970 nervous investors shared the alarm of international bankers. Many IOS punters could do no more than suffer in silence, for they had broken the currency laws of their own countries by investing in overseas stock. However, others refused to take their losses lying down. At an angry shareholders' meeting, Cornfeld was removed from control of Investors Overseas Services, squealing in protest at the loss of power over the company he had single-handedly created. He was even more upset as his own personal share of the firm dwindled in value to £4 million.

The Swiss authorities launched a fraud investigation into the conduct of IOS, and Bernie Cornfeld was ordered not to leave the country. In 1973, in stark contrast to his former lifestyle, the glib-tongued trickster was leading the humble life of an inmate in a Swiss jail, facing fraud charges. The investigation petered out, however, and Cornfeld was finally released from jail without any of the charges being pressed – thanks to an entirely new scandal surrounding the IOS's funds.

While Bernie Cornfeld was languishing in a Swiss cell, unable to control the fortunes of his old company, another American financial expert took over IOS as president. His name was Robert Vesco.

The fact that the dour, poker-faced Vesco was as far removed from flamboyant Cornfeld as chalk from Swiss cheese encouraged shareholders to trust the newcomer as their financial saviour. They could not have been more wrong.

Vesco, who lived an almost spartan life far removed from the spotlight of publicity that Cornfeld had bathed in, began a ruthless policy of translating the far-flung assets of IOS into hard cash. He managed to salvage some £150 million. The gratitude of the shareholders was short-lived, however, for Robert Vesco vanished. So did most of the money.

North American authorities issued a warrant for Vesco's arrest in 1974 but the combined resources of the FBI and the CIA could not catch him as he island-hopped around the Caribbean, increasing his ill-gotten gains by investments in the Bahamas, Costa Rica, Cuba and Panama.

He suffered one setback, however, when in May 1974 pilot Alwyn Eisenhauer flew to Panama on behalf of a group of IOS creditors. Eisenhauer marched onto an airfield where Vesco's private Boeing 707 airliner was parked and told the startled ground crew that he was taking his 'boss' on a sudden business trip.

Vesco could only watch in anguish from the balcony of his heavily-guarded villa near the airfield as his plane roared into the air and vanished in the direction of the United States. The plucky pilot claimed his bounty when the jet was sold by IOS creditors for $10 million.

Meanwhile, Cornfeld, freed from his Swiss jail cell, retired on the money that he had managed to salt away before the final crash of Investors Overseas Services. He continued to live in style in Europe, always enjoying the finest of wines and surrounding himself with the most beautiful of women. He finally moved back to California. It was the final happy homecoming of the crook who died laughing.

SKYJACKER

In smoky North American bars they sing songs about him as if he were a modern-day Robin Hood. Poems have been penned to his memory, T-shirts bear his name and newspaper editors have been deluged with letters from admiring girls pledging to be his bride.

The object of all this attention is a man who carried out one of the most heinous of crimes – skyjacking. But though he threatened to kill men, women and children, he ultimately caused harm to no-one, finally leaping into sub-zero temperatures with enough cash to make him comfortable for life.

It was the perfect crime, and it switched public sympathy away from the forces of law and order and onto the side of the culprit; the man known as D B Cooper, who has passed not into infamy, but folklore.

It was 24 November 1971, Thanksgiving Day, and the quiet little man clutching a canvas bag close to his chest in the departure lounge of Portland Airport, Oregon, attracted little attention. The airport was crammed with travellers anxious to get home to spend the holiday with their families.

The quiet man was among 150 passengers waiting patiently to take the 400-mile journey from Portland to Seattle, Washington. After acquiring a ticket under

Shadowy figure D B Cooper was just a face in the airport crowd – until his desperado skyjacking took him into the history books of terrorist activity.

the name of D B Cooper, he entered the departure lounge and waited patiently behind his dark-tinted glasses. Fifty minutes later he boarded the Boeing aircraft, still clutching the canvas bag. He placed no luggage in the hold, requested an aisle seat from the stewardess, and settled down with the bag on his lap, apparently to enjoy the one-hour flight.

About halfway through the journey he pushed the overhead button to summon a stewardess. Tina Mucklow walked down the aisle ready to take his order for a drink, when the drama began.

Instead of giving Tina Mucklow an order, he thrust into her hand a note which read: 'I have a bomb with me. If I don't get $200,000 I will blow us all to bits.'

As the startled employee of Northwest Airlines hurriedly digested the dire warning, Cooper opened the bag to show her a bomb; she could clearly identify the dynamite sticks, wiring and detonator. He never took his eyes off her as he closed the bag, watched the woman walk up to the flight deck and sat back, awaiting the response.

The Boeing, like all modern aircraft susceptible to skyjacking, was equipped with a special device which broadcast over several frequencies the message that an emergency was underway. Within seconds of Tina blurting out her news to the flight deck crew, the switch was activated. Within two minutes it had been picked up by ground control at Seattle, where a team of FBI agents, police marksmen and units of the National Guard were mobilised and placed at strategic positions.

The plane landed uneventfully at the airport, where the captain announced that disembarkation would be delayed. Amid the commotion of dismayed passengers, Cooper left his seat.

Still clutching his canvas bag, he walked through the bulkhead door onto the flight deck, where he confronted the pilot, co-pilot and flight engineer.

'Now gentlemen,' he said coolly, 'don't bother to look round.' There followed a tense twenty-minute dialogue with, first, air traffic control staff, and then a police chief, who asked for the release of the passengers before any bargains were struck.

The man was unequivocal in his demands. The passengers would be released only after $200,000 in used dollar bills had been handed over to him.

Cooper got his way, and two FBI agents dressed as maintenance men wheeled a trolley aboard. Inside it was a white package sealed with wire. Cooper ripped it open and found to his delight the money, together with the four parachutes he had demanded. He then relented and allowed the passengers to leave.

As they filed out to buses waiting to take them to the main terminal building, they were still completely unaware that a man had played a ruthless game with their lives. They thought a simple delay in transportation had held them up.

Cooper moved into phase two of his bold plan when the passengers were all safely off the plane and in the terminal. He was now captor of the flight crew only, and made further demands to the police and airport authorities. He demanded that the plane be refuelled, and he warned that he wanted flight plans to take the aircraft to Mexico. In his exchanges with the ground staff, Cooper displayed a depth of knowledge about aircraft which indicated he was neither a crank nor a lucky amateur. This escapade had been plotted to keep it simple – brilliantly simple.

When the aircraft took off again, it was shadowed by a US Air Force fighter, scrambled to track the plane to its final destination. Cooper seemed to sense the precautions that the authorities down below would take, and when airborne he told Captain Bill Scott that they were to alter course.

He was not to head for Mexico, but to veer south. He barked specific flying instructions at Scott, again indicating an astute knowledge of flying. He said: 'Fly with the flaps lowered, 15 per cent, keep the landing gear down, keep the speed below 90 metres per second, do not climb above 2000 metres (approximately 7000 feet)...and open the rear door'.

The captain did some quick mental arithmetic before telling Cooper that his instructions would mean a massive leap in fuel consumption. The skyjacker moved through the door from the cockpit to the body of the aircraft, and turned to say that the captain could land in Reno, Nevada. He told the captain to keep the bulkhead door locked.

As Cooper stood in the plane's belly, there was a huge rush of air and a deafening roar as Captain Scott activated the mechanism opening the rear door, as demanded by his sole unwanted passenger.

Scott was not to know it until he landed at Reno nearly four hours later but, in the freezing night sky, shrouded by cloud and out of sight of the shadowing military planes, Cooper had made his leap.

He left behind two of the parachutes, one intact, one in shreds. Investigators theorised later that he had ripped one apart to make a pouch for his loot that he strapped to his body. Examination of the flight's black-box recorder showed a slight increase in height at the moment he jumped – the compensation for his weight and that of his ransom. The recorder showed that Cooper jumped at 8.13 pm, just 32 minutes after leaving Seattle.

When the aircraft landed, the authorities became painfully aware that they had been well and truly duped. A contingency plan to storm the aircraft was rendered worthless when it was learned that Cooper had jumped. But they consoled themselves with the thought that the parachute jump was the one weak point in Cooper's expert plan. He had no winter clothes, no food, and wore just lightweight shoes and a raincoat for protection. His pursuers took some solace in the firm knowledge that D B Cooper had baled out over rocky, mountainous, deeply-wooded terrain that boasted sub-zero temperatures and dangerous wildlife.

There was little that could be organised in the way of a ground search over such hostile terrain. Federal aviation experts calculated that the odds on him surviving the leap in the dark were heavily stacked against him.

For two weeks after his vanishing act, exhaustive aerial searches covering vast tracts of land went on unabated. Planes with heat-seeking sensors and cameras criss-crossed the skyways over Oregon, Washington and Nevada.

There was no sign of him. Army and air force personnel joined in the ground searches – some observers cynically suggested that the objective was as much to find the loot as the man – but it was all quite fruitless. Then three weeks after the hijacking, the following letter arrived unexpectedly at the Los Angeles Times office:

'I am no modern-day Robin Hood. Unfortunately I have only fourteen months left to live. The hijacking was the fastest and most profitable way of gaining a few last grains of peace. I didn't rob Northwest because I thought it would be romantic, or heroic, or any other of the euphemisms that seem to attach themselves to situations of high risk.

'I don't blame people for hating me for what I've done, nor do I blame anybody for wanting me caught and punished, though this can never happen. I knew from the start I would not be caught. I have come and gone on several airline flights since and I'm not holed up in some obscure backwoods town. Neither am I a psychopath. I have never received a speeding ticket'.

The note – probably more than anything – helped lift the status of D B Cooper from that of villain to that of folk hero. Letters poured in to newspapers and radio stations across the United States praising the man who had managed to 'get one over on the system'.

Cooper might not have regarded himself as a modern-day Robin Hood, but the public certainly did. A university professor was engaged by FBI agents to build up a mental profile of Cooper, but his findings were never made public – lest they enhance Cooper's glamour and mystique.

Many of the 'mountain men' living in the region where Cooper jumped disregarded the letter, preferring to believe it was a spoof. Instead they embarked on wild treasure hunts amid the peaks and valleys. Clubs organised 'Cooper Loot' hunt weekends, and it became fashionable for families to spend the weekends barbecuing in the mountains, with a little light treasure hunting thrown in.

The authorities harnessed the latest technology to try to trace the money and/or Cooper's remains. Despite the letter, many high-ranking federal agents, accepting the evidence of the experts, could not believe that he survived the leap. One year after the skyjack, the FBI publicly announced that they thought D B Cooper to be dead.

Five years after the crime, on 24 November 1976, the file was closed on him, and the Statute of Limitations law meant that even if he were alive, he was a free man. The only crime he could possibly be convicted for after that was tax evasion.

In 1979 a deer hunter out on a dawn walk discovered the plastic warning sign of a Boeing 727 rear door hatch.

The message read: 'This hatch must remain firmly locked in flight'. The discovery was akin to gold being struck in the Klondike. Treasure-seekers from all over the United States poured into the nearest village to the Kelso Forest, where the sign was found. In their wake came map-makers, astrologers and souvenir sellers who certainly got far richer than the luckless prospectors, who scoured the forests and mountains in vain for the 'Cooper Loot'.

It was not until seven years after the crime that painter Harold Ingram and his eight-year-old son

Brian made a discovery which many believe proves conclusively that Cooper died in his spectacular jump. They found $3000 near a riverbank, and experts calculated that it had probably been washed down to the tranquil picnic spot by a mountain stream. The money was conclusively identified by the serial numbers as being part of Cooper's haul.

The Ingrams' discovery sparked a new wave of treasure fever. This time a group calling itself the 'Ransom Rangers' set out to try to find the rest of the skyjacked booty. But no more money was found, nor the remains of D B Cooper. 'That's the closest we ever got to him', an FBI agent remarked.

And that's the way it stays. D B Cooper pulled off one of the greatest vanishing tricks in history – if he lived long enough to enjoy it.

HORATIO BOTTOMLEY

Horatio Bottomley was a swindler without rival in his day. In a roller-coaster career of fraud, he went from rags to riches and then back to rags again. During a lifetime of financial villainy, he charmed people into parting with their money – and usually smooth-talked his way out of trouble afterwards. The phrase 'gift of the gab' seemed to have been coined just for him.

Bottomley was born in poverty in London's East End in 1860 and raised in an orphanage. His first introduction to the laws he was to flout all his life came when he got a job as a solicitor's clerk. Next came a post as shorthand writer at the Law Courts. While faithfully transcribing the devious deeds of those hauled before the bewigged judges of Victorian England, Bottomley realised where his true talents lay ...and determined to embark on the pursuit of money, women, fame and political power.

Bottomley's first foray was into the publishing business, the natural habitat of hundreds of rogues before and since. He persuaded a group of 'friends' to invest in the business and to agree to buy a number of properties, including a printing works in Devon, for the handsome sum of £325,000. His fellow directors

Orphanage child Horatio Bottomley's devil-may-care philosophy won him a life of power and esteem – but ultimately the Hand of Justice turned against him.

were less than delighted when, having parted with the money, they discovered that the properties were all owned by Bottomley himself – and were virtually worthless. The trickster suddenly found himself back in a courtroom, this time in the dock. The judge listened to the damning evidence heaped against the accused, then invited him to speak in his own defence. This was Bottomley's chance to reveal his magical talent for twisting the truth. The court was dazzled by his oratory and, after half an hour, the judge became convinced that it was Bottomley, rather than his fellow directors, who had been wronged. Clearing him of all charges, the judge even suggested that Bottomley should enter the legal profession.

This then became the *modus operandum* of fraudster Horatio Bottomley. He would set up companies and sell them at inflated prices to other companies under his control, which then went bankrupt.

His method was simple, and it was a tribute to his silver-tongued sales spiel that so many eager punters fell for it. He would start a company, declare especially high dividends and watch as the share price rocketed. He would then sell his own shares at an inflated price. In the days before strict stock market controls, this would usually go undetected. Under the pressure of his own unloading of shares, the prices would invariably plummet. At this stage, Bottomley would 'come to the rescue' of investors by offering to take over the failing firm. All he asked for was a fresh injection of funds from the poor shareholders.

During the Australian Gold Rush, Bottomley financed mining operations and made a fortune by juggling funds between his many companies – despite being served with 67 writs of bankruptcy. By 1897 he had made more than £3 million from his Australian ventures alone. The East Ender born into poverty now lived like a lord. His childhood days in an orphanage forgotten, he mixed with the highest in the land. Now married, he and his respectable wife were accepted at the dinner tables of the aristocracy. Unbeknown to his hosts and his spouse, however, he kept a succession of young mistresses in love nests throughout the country.

Horatio Bottomley had money, women and fame. What he lacked was political power. This he remedied by a string of much publicised charitable ventures, by which he 'bought' his way into Parliament. Elected to represent the poverty-stricken London constituency of Hackney South, Bottomley spent most of his time living the life of a country squire at his stately residence in Upper Dicker, near Eastbourne, Sussex.

In further pursuit of power and respectability, Bottomley returned to the world of publishing, through which he had made his first ill-gotten gains. He was instrumental in founding the *Financial Times*, which was to grow into one of the most authoritative journals of the 20th century. He also started the fiercely patriotic magazine *John Bull*, which offered its readers huge competition prizes.

There were setbacks, of course, the most dramatic of which arose from the fraudster's inveterate love of gambling. Bottomley, a racehorse owner himself, knew that the only way to be sure to win a race was to own every horse in it. And that is exactly what he decided he would do.

Bottomley scoured the Continent for a racecourse that would suit his purpose in a country where racing regulations were suitably lax. The Belgian seaside resort of Blankenberg fitted the bill precisely because the racecourse there wound its way through sand dunes and the horses were often hidden from the view of spectators and officials. On the appointed day, six horses were entered for an afternoon race – and all were owned by Bottomley.

As the time of the race approached, dozens of the schemer's accomplices placed bets on his behalf. Some of the bets were on the winner, some on the precise order in which the six horses would pass the finishing post. The six jockeys, also in the pay of Bottomley, were under strict instructions as to how to perform during every yard of the course. Then disaster befell. Just before the start, a thick sea mist blew in and obscured the entire course. The jockeys could not even see the other horses, and their shouts to one another were swallowed up in the mist. All six horses galloped to the finishing post in entirely the wrong order – thus losing the frantic fraudster a small fortune. Further disaster beset Bottomley in 1912 when he was forced to resign from Parliament after a particularly scandalous bankruptcy. The suspicion was also voiced that some of the amazingly generous prizes he was offering in the pages of *John Bull* were going straight into his own pocket.

The outbreak of World War I rescued him from political oblivion. No journal was more jingoistic than *John Bull* in supporting the war effort. Bottomley himself toured the country using his gift of the gab to boost recruiting – always charging a healthy fee for his services, of course.

At the cessation of hostilities in 1918, Bottomley was re-elected as Member of Parliament for his old constituency of Hackney South. Flushed with pride and fresh ambition, the crafty crook embarked on a string of fresh, fraudulent ventures. His past, however, was about to catch up with him.

During the war, Bottomley had instigated his biggest scam ever. The government had launched war-loan stock under the title 'Victory Bonds'. Each bond, with a redemption value of £5, cost £4 15 shillings – a high sum at the time for the working man and woman. To 'help' them, Bottomley launched a

Victory Bond Club into which the poor could pay as little as they could afford, their pennies then being invested in the £5 bonds.

Bottomley was hailed as the 'friend of the little man' as an estimated half a million pounds flowed into the Victory Bond Club. In reality, however, the crook was siphoning off about £150,000 of the paupers' cash. He used £10,000 to pay off debts, he invested £15,000 on a risky business venture of his own, and he squandered another £15,000 gambling on the horses.

When one of his former partners, Reuben Bigland, accused him of fraud, Bottomley foolishly sued for criminal libel – then dropped the case. The alarm was raised and in 1922 Bottomley faced an Old Bailey jury on a charge of fraudulent conversion of Victory Bond Club funds. This time the gift of the gab failed to sway the jurors, who took just 30 minutes to find him guilty on all counts. The judge sentenced him to seven years' penal servitude.

Released on licence in 1926, the flamboyant crook vainly attempted to restore himself to public esteem. But his fortune and his credit had long evaporated. From being one of the most respected men in Britain, he was now the most despised. In 1933 he started a new career as a concert-hall comedian but after only a few nights he collapsed from a heart attack. He died a broke and broken man.

LEONA HELMSLEY

The bell-hops quaked and reception desk staff stood to attention, their backs ramrod straight. New York's Queen of Mean, Princess of Perfection and the wickedest witch in town was on the warpath.

The little patience Leona Helmsley had was being pushed to the limit...she had been served a salad with water still glistening on the newly-washed lettuce.

Staff at the Park Lane Hotel, just across from Central Park, knew they were in for another bad day. Their boss, one of the United States' most successful entrepreneurs who had built up a formidable hotel empire, had not had her impossible standards met.

For behind the smile that beamed out from Leona's hotel adverts was a ruthless mind that seemed hell bent on damning anyone who didn't conform to her wishes. Her advertising slogan was 'The Queen Stands Guard'. Those who had been victims of Leona's back-biting, bitchiness and beratings knew that the queen also ruled the roost.

It was in the 1980s that Leona Helmsley hit the headlines as the archetypal self-made woman with a tongue as sharp as the knives that lay in precise lines in her pristine hotel kitchens. Leona's less-than-endearing qualities were admired and respected by those in the world of New York's big-bucks business. So it was no surprise that she became a media character, with interest centring on her private life.

It was Leona's love of basking in a high profile that was to lead to her downfall. If she hadn't upset ordinary, hard-working citizens by a throwaway remark, she might have won their affection for the tax fiddle she perpetrated on a grand scale.

Leona's remark is now legendary. She said: 'We don't pay taxes. Only little people pay taxes'.

There was naturally outrage across the USA, and overnight Leona, darling of the high-standard paying guest, became the Lady Macbeth of the lodging industry. Leona had at last been caught out – evading income taxes by putting personal expenditure down as business expenses. She was hurt that attitudes towards her had changed. She didn't see herself as a common criminal. But former New York mayor Ed Koch expressed his own feelings. 'She's just a wicked witch', he said.

Leona was born into a working class family in Brooklyn in 1921. Looking at the lifestyle around her and her father's desperate efforts to earn just a meagre wage, she was determined her life would be different.

'I pulled myself up', she once said. 'I adopted self-help hints. Like, I taught myself proper speech. I'd open a dictionary, pick three words, find the meaning and use them the whole day.'

Behind tax fraudster Leona Helmsley's charming smile, there lay a ruthless mind which delighted in manipulating and dominating 'little people.'

No-one could criticise Leona's efforts to make something of herself. When working as a real estate saleswoman, she thought nothing of working through the night and into the early hours just to clinch a sale. In the high-pressure, hard-dealing world of real estate she found her niche. Leona was already New York's top agent and worth around a million dollars when she met big-league millionaire property magnate Harry Helmsley in 1970. It didn't take Leona long to ease her way into Harry's empire. And she was never slow in boasting of her business skills.

She said: 'A man who is that successful in running hotels is called hard-driving, a good executive. Well, that's what I am. We employ a minimum of 10,000 people. Maybe I fired 25. I read about a man who axed 1,000 people at one network at one time. Imagine if I'd have done that. I'd have been hung.'

At its peak, Harry's empire included 27 hotels, seven of which graced New York, and a host of large skyscrapers. He had the thrill of looking out at the Empire State Building and knowing that it was all his. And because it was all his, he could shower it in patriotic red, white and blue lights every year on Leona's birthday.

Leona's business techniques couldn't be faulted. She was proud to be a perfectionist. She was proud that her hotels reflected her perfection. And she personally gave attention to every little detail. Leona would go on her hands and knees to check for cleanliness under beds. Every surface was inspected for a hint of dirt. The rigorous standards of hygiene in her hotel kitchens were maintained by Leona's impromptu prowls.

She said: 'I'm compulsive. When Harry and I were at a hotel in Ohio, I started to straighten things up. Harry said, "Stop it, this isn't even our hotel!".'

But Leona's rewards were great. Her reputation grew and high-earning businessmen and rich visitors chose Leona's hotels to rest their heads.

Even at leisure, Leona expected certain standards to be held. She went for her daily swim every morning at 6.30 am sharp. Her personal trainers were on standby. Their humiliating role was to pop seafood tidbits into Leona's mouth as she completed a length. 'Feed the fishy', Leona would cry.

Leona could be very cruel. Refusing to pay a contractor, she was quietly told that the man was struggling to look after his six children. 'Then why didn't he keep his pants on?' she replied.

No-one had seen Leona cry in public. That all changed in 1989 on the day she was sent to prison for four years and given a $7 million fine.

Leona, gathering her composure after she had been sentenced, vowed to launch appeal after appeal until she was free. And she had the money to do it, she said. Her words fell on deaf ears. Every lawyer in the United States knew she was guilty. The Queen of Mean left the dock for a low-security women's prison in Danbury, Connecticut.

Those who thought prison would be a humiliating and humbling experience for Mrs Helmsley were wrong. Leona ruled the cell block with as much style as she ran her hotels. She even had fellow inmates making her bed or doing her ironing on the promise of cash rewards or a lipstick.

Leona continued one of her best-honed skills: controlling people. Sharon Jones, a poor black woman jailed for embezzlement, agreed to be Leona's secretary in exchange for cash and gifts from the prison shop. The main work for Sharon, 32, was replying to the bags of begging letters addressed to Leona. Sharon took up a regular, friendly correspondence with one letter-writer. For some reason, this offended Leona. Acting as if she were still lording it in her hotel, she erupted into a vicious outburst. Then she reported Sharon's activities to prison authorities – even though she herself had first broken the rules by 'employing' another prisoner.

Leona claimed Sharon was gathering together material to write a book about her. Letters and pictures addressed to Leona were found in Sharon's room and she was consequently transferred to tougher, high-security jails. Sharon's lawyers protested, bitter at the way Leona had seemed to make prison warders turn a blind eye to her breach of regulations. They wrote: 'Leona Helmsley has made a practice of hiring other inmates to do favours for her throughout her period of incarceration. Rather than disciplining inmate Helmsley, Danbury staff have acted as her personal enforcement squad by misusing their authority to harass and transfer other inmates at her behest.'

Poor Sharon Jones was still languishing in jail long after Leona's release.

Astonishingly, the authorities did not consider their Queen Bee prisoner would benefit from good old-fashioned toil when serving her 750 hours of community service. Leona had originally been ordered to work at a New York hospital. She didn't like the idea of New York in the winter so, after just 20 months behind bars, she craftily wangled a cushy move. On the grounds of her age – she was now 73 – and the ill-health of her 84-year-old husband, Leona was transferred to sunny Phoenix, Arizona.

There, she was meant to continue her 'community service' by working at the city's St Joseph Hospital, now the home of her ailing husband, who had avoided prosecution altogether because of ill health. True, she spent many hours at Harry's bedside, but rumours flew that she had donated more than $1 million to the hospital to ensure her enforced time there ran smoothly. Normal obligatory cleaning work, including emptying bedpans, was not on Leona's agenda.

One member of staff remarked: 'She's treating us like this is her own hotel.'

Indeed, when Leona was not at the hospital she was able to enjoy the comforts of a $6 million mountain-top mansion she had bought nearby. Leona could proudly claim to be the only convicted criminal to carry out community service with eight staff in attendance at home round the corner.

Naturally, Leona Helmsley celebrated her escape from the rigours of New York in grand style. Guests at her 'coming out' party toasted her in champagne, and tears fell from her green eyes. She even called in to her Park Lane Hotel in New York – just long enough to strike renewed terror into the hearts of her staff. Within moments of her arrival, the news had been whispered fearfully from floor to floor of the 47-storey building.

'She's back', said one staffer, 'and it's like a volcano erupting up there. She doesn't miss a thing. The best thing to do is stay out of her way.'

The Queen of Mean was back in business!

JOHN STONEHOUSE

He was charming, good-looking and extremely polite. And, oh, that English accent! Mrs Helen Fleming, the 65-year-old receptionist on duty at the beach-side office of the luxurious Fontainbleau Hotel was highly impressed. She would long remember the English gentleman who had strolled casually up to her booth on Miami Beach. Which was precisely his plan...

Before bidding Mary Fleming farewell, the stranger passed the time of day with her and the pair enjoyed a long, uninterrupted chat. He mentioned that his name was John Stonehouse and that he was going for a swim. He wished her 'good day' and she watched as he strolled casually down to the thundering surf, seemingly just another Briton soaking up the Florida sun. Hours later his clothes were found in a neat pile on the sand. Of John Stonehouse there was no trace.

So began one of the most audacious deceptions of the 20th century. Yet it proved much more than an elaborate con trick. Stonehouse was a Labour Member of the British Parliament with personal debts of around £375,000. His business empire lay in tatters and his personal life – he was attempting to keep both a wife and mistress in tow – was a constant strain. His attempt to drag himself out of the mire by apparently vanishing off the face of the earth was nothing short of a gigantic political scandal.

Yet in 1957, when he took his seat in the House of Commons, Stonehouse had seemed destined for the very top. After serving his apprenticeship on the back benches he was talent-spotted by Labour leader Harold Wilson and put in line for fast promotion.

During the Wilson years, he rose from Aviation Minister and Technology Minister to become Postmaster General. As a privy counsellor he was entitled to be known as the Right Honourable John Stonehouse. And he was so close to the Prime Minister that Wilson lent him his private holiday home on the Scilly Isles. He was even tipped as the PM's successor.

However, when Labour lost to the Conservative Party in the 1970 elections, Stonehouse decided he could not accept either the comparative anonymity or the reduced salary of life on the Commons back benches. He began pumping money into a web of companies, including a merchant bank, in a bid to make his fortune.

Over the next four years not one of them returned a decent profit. Stonehouse resorted to the oldest trick in the book – switching funds between them to satisfy investors and auditors that all was well.

In his heart, he probably knew it couldn't last,

Debonair English MP John Stonehouse faked his own death in order to instigate one of the most convoluted fraud schemes of our time.

and in early 1974 he got wind that Department of Trade investigators were taking an interest in his companies. Even the political 'old boy' network couldn't help him now and he resolved to take desperate measures in a bid to avoid exposure. He disliked the idea of spending the rest of his life on the run so there was only one thing for it. He would have to 'die'.

Stonehouse decided that only one person should share his secret: his divorced mistress and secretary Sheila Buckley, then 28. The aim would be for them to live together in New Zealand, living off whatever money he could smuggle out from the wreckage of his businesses. There was only one snag: he had to have a new identity.

In order to achieve this, Stonehouse used a technique described by thriller writer Frederick Forsyth in his classic *The Day of the Jackal*. He first tricked a hospital in his constituency in Walsall, Staffordshire, to release personal details on two men of his own age who had died recently: Donald Mildoon and Joseph Markham.

The 48-year-old MP then obtained copies of their birth certificates and, believing Markham's background to be closest to his own, applied for a passport in that man's name. He obtained photo-booth shots of himself wearing glasses and smiling and on the back forged the counter-signature of an

Media attention and public interest focussed on the furore created by the downfall of such an esteemed Member of Parliament.

MP he knew to be dying of cancer, Neil McBride.

The application was rubber-stamped at the Passport Office and on 2 August 1974 Stonehouse picked up his new passport. He now had a duel identity and could switch his name whenever it became necessary.

Now came the second part of his plan. Over the next three months, he opened 27 accounts in his own name and a further nine in the names of Markham or Mildoon. A Swiss bank received one huge cheque credited to Mr Markham while further amounts were quietly channelled via a London account to the Bank of New South Wales. Numerous credit cards were set up in Markham's name using an anonymous address at a downmarket London hotel. Stonehouse even set up a company to help his cover story: J A Markham, export-import consultant. The only 'exports' were cash and the only customer was Stonehouse.

After a dummy run to the US, Stonehouse was ready for the real thing. He left London for Miami on 19 November 1974 with Jim Charlton, deputy chairman of one of his companies. When he failed to return from his swimming trip the following day there seemed little doubt that he had drowned. The message which was flashed from Miami Beach Police Department to New Scotland Yard read: 'John Stonehouse Presumed Dead.'

They were wrong, of course. After dumping his

Stonehouse's one-time secretary Sheila Buckley shared his deceitful plans and never wavered in her admiration and support of his character.

clothes, the MP had raced up the beach to a ramshackle building where he had hidden a suitcase containing new clothes, cash and false identity papers. He took a taxi to the airport, flew to Hawaii via San Francisco and then called Sheila Buckley to tell her their scheme had worked like a dream.

But their optimism was premature. Stonehouse arrived in Australia and was soon switching cash from a bank account in Melbourne, held under the name of Mildoon, to one in New Zealand belonging to Joseph Markham. The amounts were more than enough to raise the suspicions of bank officials and soon the police were called in. A tail was put on Stonehouse who, by 10 December, was beavering away daily, transferring funds between a string of banks. The only brief respite came with a flight to Copenhagen for a tryst with Sheila Buckley.

The net seemed to be closing, yet Stonehouse might still have bluffed his way out, had it not been for an unfortunate twist of fate.

That autumn, police throughout Australia had been briefed to look out for Lord Lucan, the English peer who had disappeared in mysterious circumstances after allegedly murdering his family nanny. When Victoria State Police asked Scotland Yard for more pictures of Lucan they received some of John Stonehouse too. The missing MP bore a remarkable resemblance to Joseph Markham.

Stonehouse was arrested on Christmas Eve 1974. He at first laughed off the questions about his false identity but a love note from Sheila Buckley found in his jacket ended the pretence. It read: 'Dear Dum Dums (her pet nickname for her lover). Do miss you. So lonely. Shall wait forever for you.'

Both Sheila and Stonehouse's 45-year-old wife Barbara flew to Australia to be at his side. Barbara quickly returned to the United Kingdom to file divorce papers but Sheila stayed on until his extradition in July 1975.

After a 68-day trial the disgraced politician was found guilty on 18 counts of theft, forgery and fraud. He was given a seven-year sentence. His mistress got two years, suspended, for aiding and abetting him.

The judge's comments at the end of the trial, that Stonehouse was an 'extremely persuasive, deceitful and ambitious man', mattered little to Sheila Buckley. She waited for him for three years – and through two heart attacks suffered in prison – to take back a bankrupt and seriously ill man.

They married in secret in 1981 and for the next few years the MP tried his hand in the world of publishing by becoming a thriller writer. He didn't make it big as an author. Perhaps his imagination couldn't compete with the astonishing exploits of the real John Stonehouse.

He died, aged 62, in 1989. Sheila said of him: 'I've

never met a man like him. John was gentle with
everybody and, in particular, with me. I'll miss him
forever.'

DEATH FAKERS

Neighbours thought little of seeing a strange man slip discreetly in and out of a widow's home. Sandra Early was still an attractive woman. She had been widowed before she reached 40 when husband Paul vanished on a boating trip. A mother of two, she bore the tragedy well. As time went by, it seemed only natural that she would begin entertaining visitors at her home on Britain's wealthy South Coast.

Insurance companies faced with a £150,000 pay-out were altogether less stoical about it. There had been no dead body or boat wreckage. A 35-day search in Spain and the Spanish waters where 38-year-old Paul Early was lost had yielded nothing. The last of three policies had been taken out, suspiciously, only a few short months before the disappearance. Now Early was missing, presumed alive.

To crack the case, the insurance companies called in top investigator Andrew Young. Mr Young and his partners at Linden Management Services in Maidenhead, Berkshire, are new-age ghostbusters. It is their brief to track down the living dead, those people who fake their deaths in order to cash in on hefty life insurance policies. Mr Young is well qualified after spending 22 years as a customs officer at London's Heathrow Airport where he investigated drug racketeers.

Initial probing by Mr Young revealed that Early was in debt after the crash of his building business. By now Mr Young was convinced that the 'missing man' was alive and well and living in Britain. A watch set up at Mrs Early's home in Bournemouth gave Mr Young the proof he needed. He realised that it was Early himself slipping in and out of the home when he thought no-one was looking.

Mr Young called for a police search. At first there appeared to be nothing out of the ordinary inside the family home – until a constable noticed one of the beds was askew. He pushed aside the bedstead and found a trap door. To their astonishment, out popped Early from a four feet deep pit beneath the trap door. He was living there until the insurance claims were settled, after which the family were planning to flee and begin a new life.

Early confessed his sorry tale to the police. He had sailed to Almeira, in Spain, in his beloved boat that he had spent five years rebuilding. There he put the boat into store and laid low. Back home, his wife claimed he was sailing to Cádiz and then returning to Britain. His father, Peter Early, also part of the conspiracy, reported his son missing on 30 November 1992. The disappearance at sea sparked an international search.

The 'dead man' arrived back in Britain just one month later. He began living under the assumed name of John Berry and went on to get a passport, bank account and a driving licence in his new name.

Early was given a four-year jail sentence at Bournemouth Crown Court in May 1994 after admitting conspiracy to obtain insurance payouts by deception. His father and wife were both jailed for 12 months for their parts in the plan.

Bogus death claims are costing insurance companies millions. Although the figure is difficult to prove, one estimate puts the sum claimed as high as £50 million a year in Britain alone, where 'vanishings' – along the lines of John Stonehouse's fake death – are a particular problem.

Linden Management Services is called in by insurance companies in Britain, the US, Canada and Europe. Mr Young says 70 per cent of the cases passed on to him are proved to be false claims. He reckons that in 12 years his company has saved insurance firms at least £60 million.

It is staggeringly easy to purchase a new identity in Britain. A trip to St Catherine's House in London gives the faker an opportunity to buy the birth certificate of someone a similar age to his or herself who has recently died. After that, it is simple to acquire credit cards and a passport. Many people with links abroad often never return to Britain after feigning their death. They will hide out in foreign countries, leaving friends, family or associates to claim from their life insurance policies. Mr Young and his partners may have to travel across the world to disprove deaths.

Shangara Singh Bogan apparently dropped dead from a heart attack on a visit to India. His brother stepped in to make claims on eight life insurance policies worth £1.2 million. Bogan had claimed he was an import-export agent in the north-east of England. In fact, he ran a corner shop. Mr Young was suspicious enough to travel to India to continue his investigations into his death. It proved a surprisingly easy case to crack.

'His relatives were everywhere', says Young. 'When I suggested Shangara was dead, they fell about laughing.'

Although he never found Shangara, the investigator gathered sufficient evidence to prove that he was not dead. The fugitive was finally discovered living in Sussex. He and his brother were sentenced to three and a half years in jail.

Priest David Asvat left his parish in Reading, Berkshire, in 1985 for a holiday in Bombay with his wife Nila. She returned alone with a death certificate, saying he had died of pneumonia and heart failure. Suspicion was aroused when it was found Asvat had eight different insurance policies which were costing him more than £1,000 each month. Mr Young embarked for India to discover that the clinic where Asvat allegedly died was run by his brother-in-law. Nila was arrested and jailed for a year. Asvat returned to Britain in 1988 to receive a three-year jail sentence.

It seemed Rodney Staples had everything to live for when he went to Thailand to marry his sweetheart. In fact, he had everything to die for, with life insurance policies worth £300,000. Once again, a bumper policy had been taken out only a few months before word reached Britain of his death from heart problems. Mr Young set out once more, this time to comb the sordid sidestreets of Pattaya. He found that Staples was well-known to locals – and owed many of them money.

With the help of two British creditors, Mr Young managed to lure Staples to a bar where he photographed him. That was enough to sink the insurance claims. Staples remained abroad, to avoid facing the courts over his deception.

Fraudsters come from all backgrounds. 'I have found a vicar, several doctors and factory floor workers', says Mr Young. 'Bogus deaths span the social and economic groups.'

Banker Adolf Pecher, of Munich, and his wife Elizabeth Guba-Pecher set their sights on a £3 million pay-out from British insurance companies through his faked death. The couple came to Britain in 1985, enticed by the prospect of the easy money to be made in property.

Pecher illegally raised nine loans on four properties, each attached to a life insurance policy. As the debts mounted, Pecher decided to 'die'. His 'widow' would reap £2.7 million, enough to pay off the £1.75 million-worth of mortgages he had acquired and still leave a tidy amount to live on.

His 'death' was a romantic concoction. He had passed away while cruising off the African coast, Guba-Pecher claimed, and was buried at sea. She substantiated the drama with a false death certificate issued by a crooked diplomat in Cairo. Pecher's two children and mother were all taken in and grieved for their loss. One insurance company paid out £150,000 but the rest were unconvinced. A simple check revealed there was no ship registered under the name that Mrs Guba-Pecher had given them. Nor could the captain be traced. This was hardly surprising, as neither had ever existed.

Yet, unbelievably, Guba-Pecher decided to sue the doubting insurance companies. She even received taxpayers cash in the form of legal aid for the battle in the British courts. She hoped for a victory in the civil courts.

At worst, she would sit it out for seven years, after which time missing people are presumed dead, and receive the money.

The audacious plan might have been successful without the wayward behaviour of Pecher, now living in Portugal. He befriended a rich and lonely widow – and relieved her of some £30,000 of life savings. It was her outraged nephew who sent information about Pecher back to London. The villain was extradited from Portugal and pleaded guilty to several charges of mortgage fraud and the attempted deception of the insurance companies. He was sentenced to 44 months in jail.

Guba-Pecher fled to Switzerland when it became clear that the game was up. She, too, was extradited and was convicted of one mortgage and nine insurance fraud charges.

Again, a fraudster had been brought back from the 'dead'. The ghostbusters had got their man!

COWBOYS

The Wild West, with its gunfights, violent gangs, horse-riding posses and saloon bar poker games, has been an endless source of romantic inspiration for Hollywood film-makers. The Western has, over the years, become an art form, and it is often the baddies who play the starring role. But how close are these film characters to the real-life cowboys on whom they were based?

Butch Cassidy and the Sundance Kid were made into household heroes through the 1970s film about their lives. But in reality they were never as famous as the film suggests.

In 1867 a child called Robert Leroy Parker was born in Beaver, Utah. His mentor and the man who taught him the fine art of rustling and horse thieving was a certain Mike Cassidy. It was Cassidy's name that Robert would later adopt when he nicknamed himself Butch Cassidy.

As a youngster Butch was rarely out of trouble. Stealing, mugging, bank hold-ups and train robbery – you name it, he did it. Inevitably, he spent some time in prison.

Eventually, when he got parole from Rawlings Penitentiary in Wyoming, he decided to set up his own gang. There were five members in all, and they

Robert Redford and Paul Newman starred as the eponymous heroes in the highly-acclaimed 1970s film romanticisation *Butch Cassidy And The Sundance Kid.*

perpetrated so many crimes that people soon began to call them the Wild Bunch. One of the gang members was the Sundance Kid.

The Wild Bunch were particularly fond of robbing trains. On one occasion they light-fingered a grand total of $30,000 from a Union Pacific express by unclipping the rear carriage and blowing open the safe aboard it with explosives.

Three more train robberies followed this one, until finally the infamous Pinkerton detectives were hired to hunt the Wild Bunch down.

The Pinkertons and other bounty hunters working for Union Pacific pursued the outlaws wherever they went. It is claimed that during all this time Butch, who was always portrayed as a cheeky, yet courteous chap, had never fired a shot directly at another man. Whenever he was being pursued he would aim at the horses instead. Animal rights activists would have strung him up from a tree.

After months of running and hiding, the Wild Bunch were forced to escape to South America. It was here, either in Bolivia or Uruguay (no one is sure), that Butch and his sidekick Sundance eventually met their fate.

Around the year 1909 they were either killed by South American troops in a huge gun battle, as the film suggests, or, as some people think, they both committed suicide.

The Sundance Kid, born Harry Longbaugh, earned his nickname when he spent 18 months in jail as a boy in Sundance, Wyoming. His face was recognised throughout the Wild West since it was always emblazoned across 'wanted' posters. In 1901 he married his girlfriend Etta Place and, to avoid the bounty hunters on his trail, they both sailed to Buenos Aires, Argentina.

Here he found rich pickings robbing banks and trains until the police got too close for comfort and he was forced to seek refuge with the local indians. He eventually met his fate alongside his partner in crime, Butch Cassidy.

One outlaw who differed from all the rest because he was such a gentleman at heart was Black Bart. He was famous because he was always well-mannered and respectful, even when breaking the law. He would never harm the people he robbed and he refused to steal money or jewellery from individuals. His targets were the safes and mailbags which were carried on stagecoaches.

His first hold-up was in the summer of 1875 when he boarded a Wells Fargo stagecoach in California. Dressed in a conspicuous white coat, with an empty sack disguising his identity, he ambushed the coach as it was climbing a steep hill. Poking out from the bushes nearby, the driver could see what he thought were the guns of Bart's accomplices. He was told to throw down the treasure box and the mailbags, which of course he did instantly since he was outnumbered seven to one.

The detective for Wells Fargo, a certain John Hume, later discovered that what everyone had believed were the accomplices' guns were in fact merely long sticks that Bart had thrust into the bushes before the robbery.

But what was even more astounding was the courtesy that Black Bart displayed during the hold-up. One woman, who was so scared that she handed over her purse without even being asked, was totally surprised when Bart gave a gentlemanly bow and returned it to her saying that he wanted only the treasure box and the mailbags, not what belonged to the passengers.

Black Bart continued to earn his reputation as the gentleman stagecoach thief for several years. However, he never earned more than $400 per robbery since most of the really valuable cargoes were carried by train.

John Hume found it almost impossible to track Black Bart because he rarely left any clues – and because instead of travelling by horse, he went everywhere by foot.

Bart was so cheeky that he even left his name and a short ditty written on a piece of paper at the scene of one of his hold-ups.

After questioning people living in the areas where Black Bart carried out his crimes, Hume managed to build up a picture of a grey-haired, bearded old man with two missing front teeth.

During one hold-up in 1882 when Bart was foiled in his attempted robbery of a stagecoach, he left behind some belongings as he made his escape. One of these was his handkerchief, which still had the laundry mark on it from the San Francisco laundry where it had been cleaned.

Hume used the handkerchief to trace down a Mr Bolton, someone who matched Black Bart's description perfectly. Bolton's neighbours had noticed that he was frequently away from home for long periods at a time, which Bolton explained by saying he had been visiting his mine.

But it was discovered that the mine did not exist – and when Black Bart's white coat and sackcloth were found in Bolton's house, John Hume knew he had at last got his man.

Bart was sentenced to only six years in prison because he agreed to return much of the money stolen during his robberies. Seen as a kindly old gentleman who happened to have an addiction to stealing, Black Bart Bolton became something of a heroic figure.

One of the most famous gunslingers of the Wild West was a mild-mannered, likable fellow called William Bonney, alias Billy the Kid. Originally from

New York, he moved out west with his family to Lincoln County in New Mexico. There he found a job as a cowboy on the ranch of an Englishman called John Tunstall.

In early 1878 Tunstall was gunned down in cold blood by two killers hired by Sheriff Brady of Pecos. Billy the Kid immediately went searching for the two murderers, and when he found them he shot them down with his two trusty Colt .44s.

This act of revenge earned him a price on his head and he was forced, for his own safety, to join a gang who eventually took care of the corrupt Sheriff Brady for good.

The governor of New Mexico, Mr Wallace, desperately wanted to get hold of Billy the Kid, whose escapades were making him a local hero. He persuaded the outlaw's former friend, Pat Garrett, to trick Billy into giving himself up in exchange for a light sentence.

When the Kid turned up in Lincoln County, he realised he had been betrayed and managed to shoot his way out of a hairy situation.

Garrett, who by now was Sheriff of Lincoln County, knew that Billy would probably seek refuge with the aid of their former mutual friend, Pete Maxwell. Garrett went to Maxwell's hideout and lay in wait for the Kid with his gun aimed at the front door. As Billy walked in, he was met with two bullets from Garrett's gun. He fell to the floor and died, having lived for 21 years and killed the same number of men.

In the same way as Butch Cassidy and Sundance, Billy the Kid would go down in history as one of the toughest cowboy gunfighters and be looked upon affectionately as a folk hero from the days of the wild Wild West.

JESSE JAMES

A century and more has elapsed since Jesse James was killed in his native Missouri, and yet historians are still piecing together the strange life, times and death of this charismatic outlaw.

Was he, as moviemakers and folklore have it, a Robin Hood of the West or merely a murderous psychopath who killed to line his own pockets? And the greatest mystery of all about this 'killer with the bayonet steel eyes', as one US newspaper described him, is whether he faked his own death and rode off into a sunset of his own choosing.

Jesse James and his brother Frank were born and raised in a tiny log cabin in Clay County, Missouri. Their mother was abandoned by her husband when Jesse was still at school and the poverty-stricken woman had to bring the boys up on her own. The family may have been poor but the mother doted on her sons and they in return seemed to retain a strong affection for her right up until death.

In 1861 the tension between the Northern and Southern states led to the outbreak of the American Civil War. Missouri was a Confederate state and, at seventeen, Jesse James joined a band of guerrillas led

Although many believed that James's crimes were morally justifiable, he was capable of heartless robbery, as this contemporary illustration shows.

by 'Bloody' Bill Anderson. The group operated under the flag and authority of the Confederate authorities but gained a notoriety for brutality which was not envied among the other soldiers of the South.

On 27 September 1864 James himself killed the leader of a Union force sent to intercept the band at Centralia, Missouri. This moved Anderson to remark with pride that Jesse was 'the cleanest and keenest fighter in the command'.

At the end of the war the Union forces claimed that Anderson's cut-throats had tortured and murdered the troops they captured. In the turmoil of a bitter war which had set brother against brother, this was hard to prove. Nevertheless, it is certain that Jesse James had blood on his hands by the time the war ended.

After the Confederate defeat, Jesse made his way back to his home town. He is said to have settled down and attended church services regularly with his mother. But the years he had spent during the war as a roving desperado had changed him deeply. In 1865 he embarked on a string of bank robberies, train hold-ups and stagecoach hijackings, which were to earn him folk hero status and a cherished reputation among the people of the South, which is still prevalent to this day.

During a long and bloody career spanning seventeen years, he was credited with plundering at

Despite outlaw Jesse James's bloodthirsty catalogue of crime, his exploits appealed to public imagination and continue to fascinate to this very day.

least eleven banks, a county fair, seven trains and three stagecoaches.

There is no doubt that James was ruthless in his exploits. In December 1869 he and his brother Frank robbed the Davies County Savings Bank at Gallatin, Missouri. While Frank held the horses outside, James approached the bank teller and asked him to change a $100 bill. While the man was busy counting out the notes, James was seized with a fit of rage. He was later to tell friends that the bank clerk resembled a Union officer who, towards the end of the Civil War, had killed his comrade in arms, Bloody Bill Anderson. James pulled out his gun, shot the man six times, scooped up $700 from his drawer and fled, 'laughing like a madman', according to eyewitnesses.

His second killing, on 7 September 1876, happened as James, by now leading a gang of desperadoes, attempted to rob the First National Bank in Northfield, Minnesota. The outlaw brutally beat the cashier, Joseph Haywood, who had said he couldn't open the safe because it had a time lock. Then, as the gang left the bank, James is said to have gone back to the dazed cashier, turned him over and shot him with a .45 bullet at point-blank range.

That would seem conclusive proof that Jesse James was something very different from a philanthropic 'Robin Hood'. But his cult status among the impoverished settlers and farmers of the

REWARD!

- DEAD OR ALIVE -

$5,000.00 will be paid for the capture of the men who robbed the bank at

NORTHFIELD, MINN.

They are believed to be Jesse James and his Band, or the Youngers.

All officers are warned to use precaution in making arrest. These are the most desperate men in America.

Take no chances! Shoot to kill!

J. H. McDonald,

SHERIFF

Jesse James's daring deeds elevated him to cult status and won him the admiration of the Southern populace – with the noted exception of the lawmen.

South – still reeling from the bitter humiliation of losing the war – continued to grow. To them, he was indeed a cavalier figure, a swashbuckling hero of the war because of the daring guerrilla raids in which he took part.

His victims were the two institutions of the day most hated by the populace: the railroads, which ran through their prime cropland, and the banks, which owned most of their property. Besides, it was commonly believed that Jesse James always had a reason for killing – that, far from being unprovoked murders, they could be easily justified on the grounds of self-defence.

But the cult status of Jesse James was finally and firmly forged upon his death. Jesse was reportedly shot dead in 1882 by Bob Ford, a bloodthirsty member of his own gang. Ford's brother Charley was an accomplice to the slaying.

According to folklore, the Ford brothers had arrived at Jesse's home in St Joseph, Missouri, supposedly to plan another robbery. The real motive for their visit, however, was their ambition to take over the gang for themselves. During their meeting, Jesse noticed that the framed inscription, 'God Bless This House' was crooked. He stood on a chair to straighten it – and was allegedly shot in the back.

Jesse was said to have been buried near to the log cabin where he had been raised. But in 1980 the grave was exhumed. Inside was found a tuft of hair, bone fragments and a .38 bullet. This was surprising, for the trademark of the Ford brothers was the type of gun they used: a powerful .44 Colt with a bullet that would stop a charging buffalo. This disparity was enough to convince some historians – and many ordinary folk – that James had had the last laugh and faked his own death.

At the time he was said to have murdered James, Bob Ford was already wanted by the authorities for murder and for his part in a train robbery. One plausible theory is that he plotted with James to fake his murder so that James could retire – an estimated $70,000 the richer.

James, in return for the favour, is said to have bribed government officials to ensure that Ford would never hang if he was caught for any murder. In 1883 he was indeed tried and sentenced to death for the murder of James; but he was given an official pardon by Missouri Governor Thomas Crittenden, a man who had publicly praised James's heroism during the bloody Civil War.

Did Jesse James make it to freedom to spend his ill-gotten wealth? Or did he die the brutal death he probably deserved? We shall probably never know the answer. Whatever the truth of the mystery, Jesse James' mother seemed unaffected by her son's removal from the scene. Not long after his 'death',

she was charging tourists 25 cents to tour the log
cabin where he was born, and to have their pictures
taken by his graveside.

LAWLESS LAWMEN

Henry Plummer looked like the answer to every law-abiding citizen's prayers. A black-bearded giant of a man, he was running for sheriff of Bannack, Montana, on a law-and-order platform in the spring of 1863, promising his voters an escape-proof jail and the tallest gallows in the country. More than that, he told the frightened miners who made up most of his constituents that his special target would be 'The Innocents', a gang of about 85 cut-throats who had terrorised the gold fields for two years.

Men who had reaped a fortune on their claims hadn't survived to enjoy it. With a death toll of more than 120 citizens on the trails out of Bannack and Virginia City, nobody dared leave either camp with a poke of gold dust on him.

When elected by a landslide victory, Plummer's first act was to call in the carpenters. Saws were soon whining and hammers resounding as his huge new gallows took shape. He then deputised three hard-faced gunfighters named Stinson, Gallagher and Ray. They carried .44s low on their hips, and the rowdiest joints grew quiet when they pushed through the saloon doors.

Plummer himself officiated at the first hanging.

The convicted horse thief plunged to eternity in a dramatic public display.

His reputation as a town-tamer established, Hank Plummer rode into the neighbouring Virginia City. It was a camp with 10,000 busy miners and one bumbling sheriff. The useless lawman happily agreed to join forces with Plummer, who promised to ride herd on both camps while the sheriff simply enjoyed his pay cheque.

The merger gave Plummer access to all records, including information on the movements of citizens and the shipment of gold by stage. The camps settled down into models of their kind, and for a good reason – miners who resisted Plummer's law were pistol-whipped into submission.

One thing still disturbed the residents, however. In the bleak Badlands outside the camps, 'The Innocents' continued to plunder and kill. Plummer told the disgruntled miners that he and his deputies were scouring the trails for the outlaws, who nevertheless always seemed to avoid his posse. And by another coincidence, the stage lines were hit when they were carrying the richest cargo.

Professional men of Virginia City's business community, headed by Colonel Wilbur Fisk Sanders, met secretly in the back room of a livery stable to study the problem. They agreed that Henry Plummer was an honest man who needed help. And when a suspected 'Innocent' named George Ives shot down a retarded boy who had harmed no one, the group made a citizens' arrest.

Ives was found guilty in miner's court and went to his death on Plummer's gallows. Until the noose tightened around his throat, he believed Plummer would intercede for him.

The sheriff sensed the mood of the camps, however. He was cautiously quiet when the citizens moved against other members of the gang: 'Club-foot George', Red Yeager, and the animal-like Boone Helm, who had once eaten his partner during a Montana blizzard.

'I don't mind dying', Yeager shouted from the scaffold, 'but I'd like to have company! The boss of this gang is your sheriff, Hank Plummer'.

Plummer and his top lieutenants surrendered meekly, pleading complete innocence. But for reasons known only to himself, the sheriff had kept one record that damned them all. Incredibly, it listed the membership of the Innocents – a total of 85 names.

Back in camp, Plummer's aides climbed stoically up the steps and onto the gallows. But according to one eye-witness report, the big sheriff heard his sentence with far less courage.

'He offered to leave the country', the witness said. 'He implored time to settle his affairs, asked to see his sister-in-law – and finally, falling down on his knees, declared to God he was too wicked to die.'

The citizens were unmoved. Bannack's law-and-order sheriff dropped to his death on his own gallows.

If Henry Plummer sounds the most crooked sheriff who ever strode the Wild West, it must be remembered that the 'good guys' were often worse than the 'bad guys' and that the long arm of the law was often as bent as a saloon-bar fiddler's elbow.

In fact, one of the most lawless lawmen of all time was a former saloon keeper, gambler, Civil War guerrilla and smuggler named Roy Bean. Backed by the Texas Rangers, 56-year-old Bean won the job of judge of the town of Vinegaroon in 1892 – because he had picked up a smattering of law from fellow poker players.

What laws Judge Bean did not know, however, he would make up. He would fine people and pocket the cash for himself.

On other occasions he would stop trials to play a few hands of poker with the accused and to serve liquor to jurors, lawyers and even the defendant.

Bean also doubled as Vinegaroon's coroner. When a local fell 100 metres (about 300 feet) to his death, Bean searched the body and found $40 and a revolver. Obviously considering the coroner's $5 fee to be insufficient, he announced: 'I find this corpse guilty of carrying a concealed weapon and I fine it $40'.

Another Civil War renegade was Wild Bill

Hickock. The former Union scout, whose real name was James Butler Hickock, turned to gambling at the cessation of hostilities and once shot dead a fellow card sharp and cheat. On the basis of this reputation as a gunslinger – highly elaborated upon, no doubt – Hickock was given the job of marshal of Abilene, Kansas.

His career as a lawman got off to an inauspicious start when he had to tackle a party of roistering drunks. He shot wildly into the mob and killed one of his own deputies.

Hickock became a popular public character when he joined Buffalo Bill's travelling stage show, demonstrating his supposed prowess with the six-shooter and telling terrible lies about his days as a lawman. With the money he earned, Hickock went on a wild spree of gambling, boozing and whoring. In 1876, at the age of 39, he was shot in the back during a poker game.

Buffalo Bill was not much better than his protegé Hickock. Born William Frederick Cody in Iowa in 1846, he became a cowboy, Indian fighter, scout, buffalo shooter and Pony Express rider. But he found his true role in life as a showman.

While on a drinking spree in North Platte, Nebraska, he was affronted to discover that no festivities had been planned for the Fourth of July, so he spontaneously advertised a talent show, urging local cowboys to show off their skills. He expected no more than a hundred cowboys but more than a thousand turned up.

Calling himself Buffalo Bill, the instant entrepreneur took his Wild West show on tour. Astonishingly, it was still running 30 years later, having visited every town in the West, as well as wowing Broadway and touring Europe. When in London, Queen Victoria was most amused by his show and awed by tales of his mythical exploits.

Buffalo Bill was encouraged in his wild boasts by a series of 121 dime novels, churned out by author Ned Buntline, packed with stories of gunfights and heroism that never happened. Buffalo Bill made a fortune during his stage days but gambled and drank away all of it. He died destitute in 1917.

Another 'hero' whose reputation was created by works of fiction was Wyatt Earp. The myth that created this most famous 'good guy' of the Badlands was hatched by author Stuart Lake, who sold a story to the Saturday Evening Post in praise of the 'bravest lawman' in the West.

In truth, Earp, born in 1848, was only briefly a lawman and it is doubtful if he ever became marshal of Dodge City or Tombstone, where his legendary exploits are reputed to have taken place.

Earp did take the job of marshal of Lamar, Missouri, but only briefly – he soon decided that hunting buffalo in Kansas was more lucrative. He returned to police work in Wichita but spent every day and night gambling and was thrown out of town.

That is how Wyatt Earp came to Dodge City and to fall in with one of the West's most misrepresented characters, James Henry 'Doc' Holliday. Far from being a kindly doctor with a mission to aid the sick, Doc Holliday was a Baltimore alcoholic with some qualifications in dentistry.

Although tubercular and a virtual walking skeleton, he had a violent temper and gunned down 14 men in his extraordinary career.

Wyatt Earp teamed up with Holliday and a fellow rogue, Bat Masterson. Masterson was sheriff of Ford County and Earp became assistant marshal of Dodge City, but that did not prevent them all enjoying a life of boozing and womanising.

It was not long before Earp was again thrown out of town and, along with his brothers and Doc Holliday, they arrived in Tombstone, Arizona, in 1879, intent on making their fortunes by fair means or foul.

Wyatt worked for Wells Fargo before being being given the job of keeping the peace in one of Tombstone's dens of gambling and vice. Although today he would be known as no more than a 'bouncer', Earp managed to install his cronies as croupiers. The gang's fortunes flourished, particularly after Wyatt's brother Virgil took over the job of acting marshal following the untimely death of the holder of that office.

Bat Masterson had remained one of Earp's associates and was recruited in 1881 to lead a posse in pursuit of raiders who had held up the Tombstone stage-coach.

The posse returned empty-handed – not surprisingly, since it was rumoured that the hold-up had been masterminded by Earp, Masterson and Holliday with the help of the notorious Clanton gang. When later that year Earp had his famous shoot-out with the Clantons in the gunfight at the OK Corral, he made sure that not a single Clanton was left alive to put the finger on him.

Holliday, who had also been a combatant in the gunfight at the OK Corral, died in 1887, aged 39, a victim of raging consumption. Earp himself moved on, quitting Tombstone to run bars in the states of Nevada and Alaska.

Even at this stage, few people had heard of Wyatt Earp as he sank into obscurity, eventually dying in Los Angeles at the age of 80 in 1929. Only after his death did Stuart Lake write the biography that immortalised the dodgy lawman as a true hero of the Wild West.

The story was immediately denounced by Wyatt's own relatives as 'a pack of lies'. But for some reason, the romantic picture of rootin' tootin' cowboys, with white hats and codes of honour, is the one that the world seems to want. Which is why books, comics, movies and television series depict some of the West's worst 'baddies' as being the most noble lawmakers who ever reached for their guns.

COWGIRLS

Far from being the the fairer sex, the women of the Wild West were no less vicious than their male counterparts. In fact, in many cases they were even tougher.

Annie Oakley, who inspired the musical *Annie Get Your Gun,* is renowned throughout the world as the sharpest shot in history.

Born on a dirt farm in Ohio in 1860, she became so famous that she would one day perform in front of Queen Victoria at a jubilee celebration show while touring with Buffalo Bill Cody's Wild West Circus.

Annie was an absolute genius when it came to using a rifle.

She used to shoot apples off the top of her pet dog's head, or hit a dime coin while holding her rifle backwards over her shoulder and aiming through the reflection of the blade of her knife. She even used to shoot cigarettes out of people's mouths at a distance of 30 yards. It was claimed that every night Annie would practice her target skills by shooting the centre of the Ace of Hearts on a playing card that her husband, Frank Butler, would hold obediently in the air. Annie Tyler was not a woman to be messed with.

Annie had a tough upbringing. She knew misfortune and suffering from an early age. One winter's day when she was just four years old, she saw her father returning home on his horse, frozen upright in the saddle. At five she fired her first gun – a cap and ball rifle – and the recoil broke her little nose. Soon she was being sent out to hunt game for the rest of the family.

When Annie was ten, her mother could no longer support her and had to send her away to work on another farm.

There she led a cheerless existence working for mean farmers who beat her regularly and even used to shut her outside on cold winter nights.

Eventually this hardship drove her away. She fled from the farm but had no money to get home to her family. She was saved by a kind man she knew only as Mr Oakley who took pity on her and paid for her train ticket home.

Vowing never to forget him, Annie later took on his name for herself.

For a while Annie supported herself by shooting game for a local hotel in Cincinnati. Then one day America's most famous rifleman, Frank Butler, rode into town and offered a prize of $50 to anyone who could outshoot him.

Annie Oakley, then just a pubescent 15-year-old girl, walked up to Butler and said she would have a go. Butler, who knew nothing of Annie's shooting prowess, couldn't help but burst out laughing. But by the time the competition was over, he realised to his embarrassment just how much he had underestimated her – for Annie had outshot him.

Frank Butler fell in love with Annie and her gun, and a year later they got married. When they got the offer to work together in Buffalo Bill's Wild West show, it was Annie who was the star and Frank who was his wife's assistant.

Annie and Frank last performed for Buffalo Bill in 1901. On the journey home their train was involved in a head-on collision and Annie was so badly injured that despite having numerous operations she was never able to walk properly again. In 1916 she was involved in another accident, this time in a car. Doctors told her she would never walk again, let alone shoot a rifle. But she proved them all wrong by appearing once in a shooting show, supported by crutches, where she shot all 25 coins that were thrown in the air for her.

In 1926 Annie died of anaemia, in Greenville, Ohio, leaving in her will more than £100,000, a fabulous sum in those days. So distressed was Frank Butler at the loss of his wife that he died of grief just three weeks later.

Unlike Hollywood's portrayal of the Wild West's infamous gunwomen as sexy, well-mannered ladies with tiny guns concealed in their cleavage, they were in reality tough, cut-throat outlaws whose sins easily matched those of their male counterparts. It was not uncommon for them to take a man to bed and days later gun him down.

They had names such as Madame Moustache, Big Nose Kate, Calamity Jane, China Mary, Poker Alice and Belle Starr.

Poker Alice (real name Alice Ivers) was the daughter of an English school-teacher. But there were no scholarly pursuits for her – she spent most of her time gambling at cards. She smoked huge cigars, wore outrageously expensive clothes and – when her husband died – opened a whorehouse. She is known to have killed at least two men. But, like most compulsive gamblers, she ended up losing all the money she ever won. In 1930 she died completely destitute at the age of 79.

Kate Fisher, or Big Nose Kate as she was known because of her startling protuberance, was a dancing girl who joined up with Wyatt Earp's gang and became John 'Doc' Holliday's girlfriend. Kate was well-matched with Doc, who as well as having the misfortune to suffer from TB, took it upon himself to carry the labels of alcoholic, gambler and killer.

Calamity Jane, born Martha Jane Caaery, lived on a diet of chewing-tobacco, liquor, swearing, cursing and fighting. She skinned mules, scouted for the US Army, served under General Custer and fell in love with the hard-drinking gambler Wild Bill Hickok.

Hickok was shot in the back during a poker game in 1876. Calamity Jane was buried near her lover when she died a quarter of a century later in 1903.

Other Wild West women lived equally brutal lives. Madame Moustache, China Mary, Blonde Marie and Dutch Annie were whorehouse madams in brothels dotted across the West. Life was tough, the men were rough, and drinking and gambling was all that these 'ladies' did when they weren't otherwise entertaining their clients.

One, Pauline Cushman, would often urge her men friends to have gunfights – and then she would sleep with the winner.

Belle Starr was an outlaw who also seemed to bring bullets raining down upon every man with whom she slept. Born to a Dallas horse-breeder in 1848, she married a native American called Sam Starr and both spent time in jail for horse-stealing.

Although many might have said that her name belied reality, Belle was fortunate enough to have affairs with countless men. She fell in love with and had the child of Cole Younger, who was in Jesse James' gang. Cole was eventually jailed for life after the famous Northfield shoot-out.

Belle also had affairs with one John Middleton and a native American named Blue Duck, both of whom were shot dead by Sam Starr. Her other lovers included a brigand called Jim Reed, who was killed, and yet another native American called Jim July. Her enviable pulling-capacity has led to modern-day cult status and in the 1980s she held the distinction of having a Top Ten pop group named after her.

Sam Starr himself died by the gun – as did Belle, who was shot in the back while she was riding her horse in 1889. Many might say that they received their just rewards – but their legendary lifestyle has certainly ensured their place in the Wild West's formidable roll of honour.

SOUTH SEA BUBBLE

It takes a very special brand of confidence trickster to bring financial ruin upon an entire country – and John Blunt was just such a man. The only ingredients he required to cause nationwide ruination were a staggering over-confidence in himself and a huge measure of ignorance among his investors – which was fuelled by greed as the fury escalated.

It was a lethal combination which devastated a massive cross-section of British society, from lords to labourers, who were taken in by the one of the biggest financial scams in British history: the so-called South Sea Bubble.

The South Sea Company was formed in 1711 with the then-generally-acceptable aim of shipping black slaves from Africa to South America. A concession to trade had been wheedled out of the French king Louis XIV, who had himself been given that right by the occupying Spanish. The agreement was instantly hailed as a milestone in improved Anglo-French relations.

For the company, however, the first few years proved grim. For a start, the available concessions were restrictive and hardly profitable. The slaves died by the hundred in appalling conditions during the voyage across the South Atlantic. And pirates made matters worse by flooding the market with slaves at rock-bottom prices.

Even the announcement that the King himself, George I, had become the company's governor failed to lift lack-lustre balance sheets.

The turn-around came when a conniving director of the South Sea Company, John Blunt, seized upon the idea of credit management, a system already being exploited well in France by a Scottish financier named John Law.

Law's theory was that governments should issue paper money through national banks instead of gold. The paper notes had to carry the pledge that they could be exchanged for gold at any time – otherwise the financial community would have no confidence in them. But once confidence was established, a government could simply print more notes whenever it was short of cash.

It seemed too good to be true, which of course it was. Today we know that such a policy is doomed to end in rampant inflation. But at the time the likes of John Law (who virtually single-handedly ruined the French economy) and John Blunt saw their schemes as economic miracles which could not fail.

Blunt persuaded his fellow directors at the South Sea Company to embark on a business plan in which they would take total responsibility for England's National Debt (the £50 million the government had borrowed from its own citizens). They would even pay £8 million for the privilege.

The plan went like this. Anyone with, say, £10,000-worth of government bonds could redeem them at the usual, modest rate of interest. Or instead, one could choose to reinvest in South Sea stock with its promise of fabulous rewards. Each company share would be launched on the market for £100, and so the £10,000 investor would receive 100 spanking new printed shares.

But what if the publicity and excitement generated by this imaginative new venture was such that there was a huge demand? Shares would then naturally rise in price – perhaps even double to £200 apiece.

The next £10,000 investor to come along would need only 50 shares from the company, leaving another 50 to sell to someone else. The instant profit for the company would amount to £10,000. The key was to keep the sale price of the shares rising so that there were always plenty of new investors ready to jump on board.

The idea went before Parliament on 22 January 1720 and, despite noisy objections from the Bank of England, which saw its own role being eroded, it was approved by a majority of four votes. Supporters believed the deal was good for the country because the government would pay the company only 4 per cent interest on loans rather than the present 5 per cent.

Within a quarter of a century, it was claimed, the National Debt slate would be wiped clean and England would once again be able to trade with the world unfettered by the financial millstone around her neck.

Few of the investors in this new scheme really understood how credit worked. But at the time they didn't care. They didn't so much jump on to the band wagon; they more like fitted it with a turbo-charger. And at first it seemed they were right. The share price quickly rocketed to £400 before a few jubilant early profit-takers damped it down to a steady £330.

Within a matter of weeks widows and pensioners were retrieving their meagre life savings from beneath mattresses to plough into the South Sea Company. Farm workers and fishermen rushed to buy their stake before the price spiralled again, and the landed gentry poured in every last penny they could find. Some people even remortgaged their homes or borrowed from more circumspect friends to increase their exposure to this seemingly amazing, no-risk wonder company.

The frenzy persisted even when three months after launch Blunt revealed another 20,000 shares were up for grabs. This was an illegal move, since parliament had decreed the only shares that could be sold were remainders left after government creditors and pensioners had received their full allocation.

It didn't seem to matter. The new stock sold for £300 per share and a further 10,000 floated later in the month went for £400. Many people took their lead from the King who had let it be known of his own £20,000 investment. George sold his stake for a handsome £86,000 profit early on and was so pleased with John Blunt's performance that he awarded him a knighthood.

Incredibly, none of the money that came in was reinvested by the South Sea Company. No-one stopped to think that it should be put to work – making things or providing services for consumers. Directors of the company wallowed complacently in the belief that if they needed more money, they just printed more shares.

Before 1720 was out, a host of other entrepreneurs were taking a slice of the action with their own hastily-formed companies. Most of these were illegal because they were trading without a royal charter having been awarded to them.

But both the authorities and the general public were too busy getting rich quick to care. Hence anyone could buy shares in pirate-proof ships or wheels claiming to produce perpetual motion. Investors could get into the jackasses-from-Spain import business or silkworm production in Chelsea.

One sincere-looking entrepreneur even sold shares in a company whose declared aim was 'carrying on an undertaking of great advantage but no-one to know what it is'.

He promised an annual return of £50 on every £1 invested and on his first day pocketed £2000 from excited punters. The man vanished that evening, his 'undertaking of great advantage' complete.

By August 1720, the South Sea Company had taken more than £8 million from its shareholders. But because many had bought under hire purchase-type agreements, there was £60 million worth of payments still to come in. By now some of the new 'Bubble' companies were starting to go bust – a factor that further slowed the flow of funds into Blunt's coffers.

The mood was imperceptibly changing but Blunt failed to see it. He ordered the prosecution of four large rival companies which, he alleged, were trading without a royal charter.

The courts backed Blunt and the companies' stock became worthless. Rarely in the field of great financial disasters has anyone misjudged the might of market forces so badly. Investors in the four bankrupt companies decided to solve their personal financial problems by selling their best assets – South Sea Company Shares. Suddenly, instead of everyone wanting to buy, numerous big 'players' wanted to sell. Word spread and smaller investors picked up the vibes. Confidence, the factor that drives any credit economy, was taking a massive nose-dive.

Within days, South Sea shares were in free fall. Their value was reduced from £900 apiece to £190 and thousands of people stared ruin in the face. The Duke of Chandos saw £300,000 disappear almost overnight and poets such as Alexander Pope and Matthew Prior also saw their life savings trickle away. Civil unrest loomed and at one point the King even considered bringing over his German troops from Hanover in case of riots.

Outraged MPs and the public felt swindled and they demanded a Guilty Man. Blunt was the obvious option and he was hauled before a parliamentary committee – to be told his personal £185,000 fortune would be reduced to £1000.

LADY ABERDOUR

Being born into a comfortable middle-class English family was not enough for Rosemary Aberdour. The plump only child knew she was destined for better things. And even when she was still part of the village community of Wickham Bishops, Essex, Rosemary wore a smile that seemed to hide a thousand secrets.

It was a smile that was to see her through three years of lies, fraud and fantasy, as the daughter of a doctor and medical secretary lived the life of an aristocrat. She became rich off the backs of others' hospitality – a charitable generosity which catapulted the former Sunday School helper into an existence of sheer opulence.

There were lavish parties, expensive cars, made-to-order jewellery, luxury homes, vintage champagne and all the other trappings of a millionaire lifestyle. And that's just what Rosemary led – all under the title of Lady Rosemary Aberdour, a title she gave herself. At one point, Rosemary spent nearly £1.5 million in three months alone. And all the while, she spoke of an inheritance which existed only in her mind.

Rosemary had decided at an early age that she was good at handling other people's money. While living at home, she had helped raise funds for her local parish church. But already she was dreaming and scheming of unlimited funds of her very own. Rosemary was telling friends she was due to come into money. Even she could not have imagined how much, or indeed just how it was going to come her way. But as always, Rosemary wore her secret smile and knew fate would treat her kindly.

It was when she arrived in London that Rosemary set about her master plan of having at her disposal as much money as she could lay her fingers on. She took a course in book-keeping, a skill which was to come in exceptionally useful when she was in a position to make the books balance greatly in her favour.

That opportunity came in November 1986 when she successfully applied for a £20,000 a year book-keeping job at London's National Hospital in Queen's Square. The hospital had a development fund, in the form of a charity launched to raise £10 million to build a new wing.

Rosemary knew she was just the person to use any donations wisely – on herself. But in the eyes of charity chairman John Young, Rosemary was a highly desirable asset to his campaign. She came highly recommended with an impeccable background and enthusiasm which could not help but impress. After organising a charity ball at London's Guildhall, attended by the Princess of Wales, Rosemary knew this was the glittering life she wanted to lead. She set

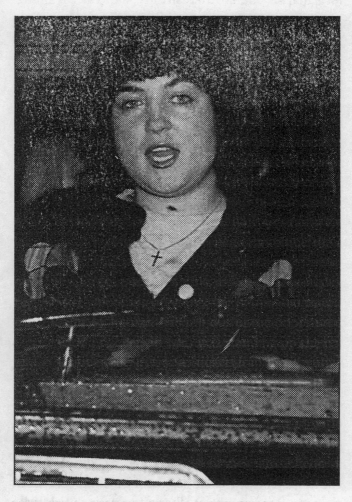

The champagne lifestyle of the self-styled Lady
Rosemary Aberdour hid the lonely reality of a
woman who tried to buy love.

about achieving it earnestly.

In July 1987 Rosemary's months of devotion to duty paid off. She was promoted to the charity's deputy director. It was a position of great trust. Rosemary was to bank all the cheques that came into the National Hospital Fund and look after the accounts. Hundreds of thousands of pounds passed through her hands. And once Rosemary realised she had got away with stealing £500 to take herself away on holiday, there was no stopping her. She simply took the cheques for herself and fiddled the books.

The real golden opportunity came when Rosemary was asked to become chairman of the Queen's Square Ball, a separate fund-raising committee. The contents of its bank account were only needed when the date of the annual ball came around. The rest of the year, it came under no scrutiny. Rosemary had all the time in the world to deposit money stolen from the National Hospital Development Fund into the Queen's Square Ball account – and to use the account as her very own nest egg. She regularly stole cheques received in the post, amounting to anything between £20,000 and £100,000 at one time.

Not content with having one source of illicit income, Rosemary started to forge the signature of the charity's director Richard Stevens. She now had fraudulent cheques to increase her spending power. At last, money was no object.

When Rosemary wanted a new car, she bought one: a £70,000 Bentley. And just as always, Rosemary had an answer. When asked about her purchase, made on the Queen's Square Ball account, she told top-notch car dealers H R Owen that the millionaire's car was to be a raffle prize at the ball.

Then there was the £171,000 of charity cash which Rosemary spent at top jewellers Boodle & Dunthorne, and the luxury new home in Kensington. She even sent her chauffeur to top people's store, Harrods, to buy fillet steak for her dog Jeeves.

It was incredible that no-one ever delved too deeply into Rosemary's spending. But if they did, she had answer for that too. 'I'm an heiress', she would reply coyly. 'I have an inheritance of £20 million.'

And no one disbelieved her. John Young said Rosemary had a royal air about her and a 'great presence'. The fake Lady Aberdour even cheekily arrived for work in her chauffeur-driven Bentley, waving at Mr Young regally.

In fact, there was no end to the fake Lady's nerve. She wrote to Richard Stevens enclosing a cheque for £100,000. This, she said, was her gift towards a new hospital ward. And her trust fund had given her permission to make donations totalling £500,000 towards this worthy cause over five years. Rosemary asked that her donation be received 'anonymously'.

This was hardly surprising when she had stolen the money from a charity headed by Mr Stevens himself. Rosemary loved the high life. There was no limit to her spending. She would go on wild sprees with her credit cards and think nothing of spending £30,000 on a weekend shopping jaunt. And she soon acquired a new circle of friends – people she felt would not question her aristocratic status too closely.

But it was the extravagant parties for which Rosemary became renowned. Entering into the spirit of being a member of the aristocracy, a respected socialite, and now a generous benefactor, she entertained lavishly.

Just one of her many parties at her London home had a Caribbean theme. She employed professional party organisers to make sure every attention was paid to detail. Guests, wearing grass skirts and loud shirts, arrived to find live lobsters in tanks of water, bars with Caribbean roofs made out of specially imported materials, two tons of sand, palm trees and champagne spouting from showers. It had taken seven days to 'build' the party, at a cost of £40,000. As one partygoer said: 'It was Rosemary living a dream. It was her way of going to the Caribbean for the weekend.'

Rosemary was never to explain why she decided upon Lady Aberdour as her aristocratic pseudonym. But there was one particular family who felt she had a lot of explaining to do – the REAL titled Aberdours. They only became aware of an impostor when a Sunday newspaper wrote about Rosemary. The writer thought it too audacious to question her face-to-face about her family roots. So he looked the family up in the aristocrats' directory *Debretts*, found the Aberdours and placed Rosemary as being the 21st daughter of the Earl of Morton.

The Countess and Earl of Morton were somewhat anxious that their family name was being taken in vain. Indeed they wrote to *The Sunday Times* and told them so. They were no less anxious when they received a reply saying there was obviously another branch of the family.

'We were slightly annoyed,' said the countess. 'It was a silly reply. There is no-one in the family called Lady Rosemary Aberdour.'

Even when the real Lord and Lady Aberdour found out that someone was living a lie and using their name, no-one pursued investigations which would have revealed Rosemary's barefaced fraud.

'There is only one Lady Aberdour, and that's my wife Amanda', said a bemused Lord Aberdour, the earl's son. 'This woman is definitely a fraud.'

It was now taking all Rosemary's nerve, not only to maintain her fake existence, but to avoid discovery over rapidly-dwindling charity funds at the National Hospital. A scheduled visit from auditors meant

Rosemary had to put in overtime – to balance the books. She had to adjust figures, produce forged documents and transfer cash. She even raised an overdraft on the Queen's Ball account. The auditors did not notice anything was amiss.

'It was all done with stunning skill', said John Young. Mr Young was later to fall victim of Rosemary's quick-thinking. She forged his signature to get her hands on even more cash, and when a building society manager queried it, she told them that 'poor Mr Young' suffered from Parkinson's Disease, which made his hands shake.

By now, Rosemary knew deep inside that all the money in the world could not buy love or friends. She had no real friends, just hangers-on. And even they were beginning to tire of the party merry-go-round. It was always the same crowd of people. Rosemary determined to put on a party more outrageous than the last, desperate to be the centre of attention. It was a sad fact, however, that guests at her parties now comprised staff and the most casual of acquaintances.

'She left all her parties early', said one partygoer, Hamish Mitchell. 'It was as if she wasn't having a good time'.

Ever-blinkered to life's harsher realities, poor-little-rich-girl Rosemary decided to cheer herself up with the biggest party ever. In fact, it was a fortnight of parties. Venue for the two weeks of total self-indulgence was Thornton Watlass Hall, a magnificent country estate in Yorkshire. Every night, the guests sat down to a gourmet dinner. There was live entertainment by top cabaret artists, firework displays, vintage car races and, of course, the best champagne permanently flowing.

This all astonished Thornton Watlass Hall's estate manager, Tim Mudd, who had expected 'Lady Aberdour' to be a genteel, elderly member of the nobility, renting the place for a deserved period of rest and relaxation.

Perhaps living such a complex lie began to take its toll on Rosemary. Or perhaps she at last realised that the good life would come to an end. Whatever her reasoning, Rosemary was determined to give up her 'career' with as much extravagance as she had pursued it. She rented a London penthouse at an annual fee of £123,000. The luxury apartment had its own swimming pool and was to be the venue for yet more of Rosemary's flamboyant hospitality. Then she embarked upon the spending spree of a lifetime.

There were two £40,000 parties – first a Star Trek 'Voyage of Discovery' party which Rosemary hosted, followed by a birthday party for a friend – a medieval banquet at Conwy Castle in Wales. Guests were flown in by helicopter. There was the Teddy Bears' Picnic which cost £70,000 to stage at the top London hotel, Claridges. Personal indulgences included a

£9000 'RUA' personalised car number plate for her Mercedes sports car, £78,000 to hire a yacht, £34,000 worth of vintage champagne and £54,000 on her favourite flowers, white lilies.

At the height of Rosemary's frenzied spending in December 1990, she was getting through £15,000 every single day. In just three months, she went through £1,350,000.

By April 1991, Rosemary had all but exhausted the charity donations she had appropriated. For the first time since she became the Good Life Lady, she began to owe people money.

A few weeks later, Rosemary knew it was all over. Charity director Richard Stevens found a letter in one of Rosemary's office drawers. It bore the forged signatures of both himself and John Young. The letter was to the Abbey National Building Society, asking them to transfer £250,000. 'It was a very good forgery', admitted Mr Young. He confronted Rosemary. Cool to the last, she told him she had 'cash flow' problems and that the matter would be sorted out that very afternoon. It never was. Rosemary boarded a plane for Brazil and people started having serious doubts about their socialite friend and devoted charity worker.

As Mr Young was later to say: 'The alarm bells rang.' A daily newspaper received the tip-off that Lady Rosemary Aberdour had 'done a bunk'. Soon the swindling impostor, who had stolen around £3 million of charity funds, was headline news.

After a week in Rio contemplating her fate, Rosemary was persuaded by her family and boyfriend Michael Cubbin to return to face the music, and she flew back to London to give herself up to the police.

Having spent six months on remand – where she had to get used to a new title: 'Prisoner Aberdour, number TT184' – Rosemary appeared in court to plead guilty to seventeen charges, including five of theft and eleven of obtaining property by deception. She had stolen and spent exactly £2,700,000.

Prosecuting barrister Brendan Finucane said Rosemary's spending had become an addiction. 'She spent all the money on such a grand scale', he said. 'It was like the compulsion of a gambler. The money all went. She needed to fuel these fantasies she had. She continued to do it until, by chance, she was stopped.'

People like Michael Wainwright, of jewellers Boodle & Dunthorne, attended the hearing to learn more about the woman they had trusted. 'I went along out of curiosity', he said. 'I felt she had let us down – we felt very used. We had treated her like one of the family.'

When asked by the press why Rosemary had led the life she did, those in her party circle shrugged, saying that, in her own mind, Rosemary believed she was an aristocrat and therefore lived like one.

Rosemary was sentenced to four years in prison. Newspaper reports labelled her 'Snooty Big Spender', 'The Girl Who Tried to Buy Love', and 'Phony Aristocrat'. And the Essex girl returned to Essex to serve her time, at Bullwood Hall prison.

Meanwhile, the National Hospital was left to sort out the monumental financial fraud she had perpetrated. Managers of the National Hospital Development Fund and the Queen's Square fund refused to accept the mess had been of their making. They blamed building societies and banks for failing to act the moment suspicions had been aroused.

Under threat of legal action, the building societies involved paid back £1.5 million pounds; the banks nearly £1 million. The charity was determined to recoup as much of its loss as possible. It served writs on those who had provided services or goods in return for their stolen money and fraudulent cheques. As one party organiser said: 'It all got pretty nasty.'

Rosemary's furniture and paintings went back to the shops that had sold them and the money was refunded. Other possessions fetched around £100,000 at a sale organised by top-notch London auction house Christie's.

The Charity Commission was called in to investigate how it had all happened. Their findings were simple: Rosemary had used charity donations to her own benefit, apparently answerable to no one. And her cunning accountancy meant auditors had failed to notice any discrepancies. National Hospital Development Fund director Richard Stevens, left to become a fund-raiser for Southampton University. Chairman John Young survived the scandal and became president of the fund.

He later said: 'We shall never know how much Rosemary's fraud was planned. But she took people into her confidence and conned everyone, including her friends, family and fiancé. She was very cunning'.

Rosemary's actions directly responsible for the passing of a new law concerning charity money. The 1992 Cheques Act means such forgery supposedly became impossible.

Rosemary served two years of her sentence and was released in October 1993. The National Hospital's long-awaited new wing, with its eight wards, opened three months later.

Fiancé Michael Cubbin, a helicopter pilot, stood by Rosemary. They made their home in a village in Oxfordshire. Rosemary was lucky to have a man like Michael. All her so-called friends had deserted her. Promises of million-pound book and film deals about her life had evaporated. The party really was over.

Michael and Rosemary married in November 1994. The wedding took place at Rosemary's local church, back home in Wickham Bishops. At 32 years of age, Rosemary had finally settled into an ordinary, honest life. The former 'Lady Aberdour' had found that money really *can't* buy love.

Ironically, however, once her bizarre double life came to an end, Rosemary finally did find true love and lived happily ever after.

PIRATES

They sought a life of adventure and danger. And what better way to fulfil their dreams than a life on the high seas, plundering enemy ships? No-one admitted the sea-faring scallywags were pirates, breaking the law at every turn of their vessels. And the reward for those rascals was two-fold. They earned admiration from their sovereign for serving their country well. They also lined their pockets with the 'gratitude' shown them.

All children love to play pirates. Their legendary reputation as romantic, swashbuckling, plank-walking rogues cannot help but capture the imagination. But back in history, they took their buccaneering seriously.

The word 'pirate' comes from the Greek *peiran*, meaning 'to attack'. Between 1550 and 1750, thousands of these attackers sailed the seas in the West Indies, Mediterranean and off the coast of Africa. Many of them were former British sailors who knew they would receive royal blessing for hijacking ships coming from France, Portugal or Spain – all their country's enemies.

Most famous super-pirate of all was Francis Drake who was knighted for making his dear Queen Elizabeth I very rich indeed. The queen turned a blind

Mary Read (above), who assumed a man's identity to travel with 'Calico Jack' Rackham's crew, and proved herself to be as tough and brave as any male pirate.

THE
TRIALS

Of Eight Persons

Indited for Piracy &c.

Of whom Two were acquitted, and the rest found Guilty.

At a Justiciary Court of Admiralty Assembled and Held in Boston within His Majesty's Province of the Massachusetts-Bay in New-England, on the 18th of October 1717. and by several Adjournments continued to the 30th. Pursuant to His Majesty's Commission and Instructions, founded on the Act of Parliament Made in the 11th & 12th of KING William IIId. Intituled, *An Act for the more effectual Suppression of Piracy.*

With an APPENDIX,

Containing the Substance of their Confessions given before His Excellency the Governour, when they were first brought to Boston, and committed to Goal.

Boston:

Printed by B. Green, for John Edwards, and Sold at his Shop in King's Street. 1718.

Although piracy was potentially a hanging offence, in practice many convicted pirates were treated leniently for the sake of diplomatic appearances.

eye to the dishonourable ways of her 'daring little pirate' and he became a regular and favourite visitor at her Court.

It was no wonder Drake was a hero to the English and arch-enemy to foreign sailors. He returned to England after a voyage of discovery in 1580 with treasures valued around £600,000 aboard his ship *Golden Hind* (about £20 million in modern terms).

When the *Golden Hind* sailed up the Thames Estuary that year, she left behind a trail of unparalleled plunder. After ravaging the coasts of Chile and Peru and looting the shipping of the Philippine Islands, Drake was forced to jettison half his booty just to keep his ship afloat on the voyage home. Yet his profits were still a fantastic 4700 per cent of the cost of his voyage.

Whether we choose to call them pirates, corsairs, privateers or plunderers, Drake and his fellow maritime marauders toured the seas, leaving mayhem in their wake. The notorious Jolly Roger flag, with its skull and crossbones, soon became their trademark, hoisted high above every raid. With commissions from Queen Elizabeth I to explore and develop new territories, their real aim was to steal as much Spanish gold and sink as many Spanish galleons as possible before that country's inevitable declaration of war against England.

One pirate, John Avery, used flags to his very best

advantage. Sailing off the coast of Guinea, Avery took his Jolly Roger down and flew the English flag in its place. The natives, seeing a 'friendly' flag flying merrily in the breeze, rowed out to do some trading with their visitors. But the moment they climbed aboard they realised they had been tricked. Avery dispatched them all, ordering them to leave their hoard of gold behind. It was a pirate victory without a single act of violence. In fact, Avery, who originally went to sea as the mate of a trading ship, earned a reputation as the most gentlemanly of pirates.

There was no stopping him after he successfully led a mutiny in 1694. But all his plundering was done by smooth-talking rather than by striking blows. He once even tricked fellow pirates into handing over their haul by convincing pirate captains that instead of constantly fighting over how ill-gotten treasure should be shared, they should entrust it to him for safe-keeping. Of course, they never saw it again.

Despite his wily ways, Avery, the pirate who never drew his sword, eventually died in poverty in his home county of Devon.

If Avery was the most peace-loving of pirates, then Captain Charles Vane was the cheekiest. In the early 1700s there were around 2,000 established plunderers. Vane was one of the most daring. With fellow pirate Henry Jennings, Vane gathered together five ships and 300 men. They then caused a diplomatic incident of monumental proportions by stealing 350,000 pieces of gold from a Spanish salvage crew. The crew had spent months raising treasure from a wreck sunk by a hurricane off the Bahamas.

Vane showed his nerve, too, when Britain, under pressure from other countries, sent fighting ships to the Bahamas to try to end piracy once and for all. Vane was ready and waiting. Using the old trick of flying friendly flags, Vane's ship sailed straight towards his enemy. The British ships, seeing a smartly dressed captain saluting them, simply returned the salute and sailed on. It was only when they got to shore that they realised their pirate prey had slipped away from under their very noses. Even when Benjamin Hornigold, an old comrade of infamous and evil pirate Blackbeard, was commissioned to track Vane down, the impudent rascal disappeared. He was never seen or heard of again.

So colourful a reputation did Vane's era of piracy earn that it was to be immortalised by such authors as Daniel Defoe and Robert Louis Stevenson. It is not surprising, with such characters as Vane's former quartermaster John 'Calico Jack' Rackham around.

Rackham built up his own pirate crew after being drummed out of Vane's service for cowardice. Much to the disgust of other pirate ships, Rackham allowed two women to join him. The women, Mary Read and Anne Bonny, were to become known as 'female pirates', earning themselves mention in Defoe's book *General History Of Pirates*. Defoe spun a romantic tale of Anne and Rackham's great love affair, with Mary finding her true love on board. He even wrote a ballad in their honour:

With pitch and tar their hands were hard,
Tho' once like velvet soft,
They weigh'd the anchor, heavy'd the lead,
And boldly went aloft.

Historians claim the women were probably of ill repute, taken on board for the pirates' pleasure. Romantics prefer the story in which Anne met Rackham, fell desperately in love and then disguised herself as a man to join him on board. She proved herself as tough as any man, even taking part in attacking other ships.

The story has it that Anne met her female sea companion when Rackham captured the pirate ship on which Mary was sailing. The women became firm friends and fought on the high seas together.

When an armed vessel was sent from Jamaica to take in Rackham and his motley crew, Anne and Mary fought to the end. When brought to court in Jamaica in 1720, the two women used female wiles to trick the judge. They begged to be spared, both claiming they were pregnant. 'My Lord, we plead our bellies', they cried. The judge believed their lies.

Mary Read and Anne Bonny thus became heroes

in piracy legend. They were two convicted pirates who had managed to escape the gallows.

Even pirate leaders were favoured by the law – especially if they were 'gentlemen'. Such notables as William Hawkins, Sir Richard Neville, William Hawkins and Thomas Cobham, the son of Lord Cobham, warden of the Cinque Ports, appeared before the Privy Council in the 16th century on charges of piracy. For the sake of diplomatic appearances, they walked away with nothing more than reprimands.

The whole of the principality of Wales was virtually a pirate kingdom, with the Augustinian priory on Bardsey Island under perpetual orders 'to be at all times ready to deliver to all such pirate victuals and necessaries, receiving for the same a large recompense, such as wine, iron, salt and spices'. Even the Admiralty's own vice-admiral, Sir Richard Bulkeley, regularly entertained pirates of various nationalities at his mansion outside Beaumaris, on the island of Anglesey.

With churchmen, politicians, aristocrats and royalty all covertly supporting the waterborne brigands, it is hardly surprising that their trade thrived throughout the seven seas. In fact, the finest seamen were for more than a century all pirates. Not least of them was a Genoese sailor who fought under the French flag to loot Venetian galleys bound for

England. But that was before he took a commission from the king of Spain and became renowned as the world's greatest navigator and discoverer of the New World – Christopher Columbus.

RONNIE BIGGS

The funeral marked more than just the death of one of this century's most infamous villains. It brought together, for the first time in many years, the surviving gang who had perpetrated one of the most notorious crimes in British history. No one was surprised, however, at one notable absence. But if Ronnie Biggs couldn't be there in person, he was certainly there in spirit.

Ronnie quietly raised a toast to the memory of fellow thief Buster Edwards. And, from the long-distance safety of Brazil, he sent his feelings of 'sorrow and affection' over his untimely death.

Edwards was laid to rest on 10 December 1994. Driven to bouts of black depression, he had hanged himself in a lock-up garage close to his flower stall at London's Waterloo Station.

His death put back onto the front pages of newspapers what is forever to be known as The Great Train Robbery. But while Edwards had considered himself the most affected by the robbery – he never recovered from his nine-year prison sentence – Ronald Biggs has good reason to consider himself the luckiest.

Biggs was always the most slippery of the Great Train Robbers. More than 30 years after his gang got their hands on £2.5 million pounds from a mail train, he was still living in Rio de Janeiro, out of the clutches of British police and unlikely ever to come to justice. For Ronnie, crime DID pay. And people still see him as as a villainous hero, the great survivor of the crime of the century.

Despite being the best-known of the Great Train Robbers, Ronnie's reputation as a 'Mr Big' is misplaced. Indeed, not only did he play a relatively minor part in the crime, but he was also a last-minute recruit to the conspiracy.

What Ronnie did have when he was approached to join a 'big job' was the yearning to get his hands on enough money to end his decorating days forever. Income from petty thieving was not enough. In his dreams he saw a life of luxury just waiting for him and his pretty wife.

So when the chance came up, he took it, never for once realising he was about to be part of a robbery that would become criminal legend.

The plan that was hatched, over 18 months before the mail train hold-up on 8 August 1963, was near-perfect. According to the criminal fraternity, old banknotes from all the banks in Scotland were sent by night train to London to be destroyed.

Such was the information gleaned by Ronnie and his gang that they knew there were usually four Post Office staff in the so-called High Value Packages Coach carrying the money.

That particular coach was always next-but-one to the diesel engine but the one in the middle contained only parcels – and was never manned.

Of course, not even the gang's informants could guarantee just how much money was up for grabs. But already Ronnie was planning a future funded with untold riches from just one night's illegal activity. As the months went on, the train robbery gang grew and plans became more detailed.

Location for robbing the train was set at Bridego Bridge, which carries the main Scottish railway line over a lonely country road through Buckinghamshire farmland. Endless patience night after night had rewarded the robbers with the knowledge that the train was ripe for ambush from the bridge at 3 am. The gang worked out that two warning lights could be switched.

One, several hundred yards up the track, would cause a train to slam on its brakes; another, closer to the bridge, would bring the train to a full stop. After delegating certain members to ensure lines to trackside emergency telephones and nearby farms and cottages were cut at the crucial time, the gang was set for the big night.

That came on 7 August 1963 when Biggs, the robber with the charming smile, and the rest of his colourful band set off from their base, Leatherslade Farm, to travel the 26 km/16 miles to Bridego Bridge.

Charismatic criminal Ronnie Biggs remains a popular anti-hero to this day. In the 1970s his cult status led him to cut a disc with the notorious punk rock band The Sex Pistols.

No one will ever know the full company Biggs kept that night. It has been rumoured that at least 15 crooks put their heads together for the Great Train Robbery. Only ten were to see the inside of a jail for an extended time.

No one will ever know, either, what was in Biggs' mind as he nervously joked with the likes of Bruce Reynolds, Charlie Wilson, Tommy Wisbey and Gordon Goody – all London villains with a thirst for the good life.

In place at the bridge, final instructions barked out, the gang sat and waited. At precisely 3 am they saw the train approaching. Shouts of 'Go! go!' echoed through the air as signals were changed, phone lines cut, and coshes and other arms were taken up.

Train driver Jack Mills had no reason to be suspicious when he saw a signal glowing amber for caution. He brought the train down to 30 miles per hour. Further on, he saw the red signal. Co-driver David Whitby got down from the train to telephone the signal box to find out what was going on. He called back to Jack that the first phone he tried wasn't working and set off to the next one.

Before he could say any more, Whitby was manhandled by two of the gang and bundled back onto the train.

Meanwhile, Mills was attacked from both sides and struck twice on the head. The gang was later to swear that physical injury was not part of their plan; that something had gone badly wrong. And no gang member has ever owned up striking those blows – an attack from which Jack Mills never recovered. His health declined as a result of his ordeal and he died six-and-a-half years later.

Unaware someone had overstepped the mark, the rest of the gang moved in swiftly. They separated the engine and two front coaches. Inside, Jack Mills was ordered to drive them closer to the bridge. With postal staff ordered to back off, the gang now methodically looted the mail coaches. Two unloaded 120 of the bags while the others formed a chain, transferring them to a waiting van.

In all, the gang made off with around two and a half million pounds – £2,631,784 to be exact.

The robbers made their way back to Leatherslade Farm where they piled up their haul in the living room. Their joy at pulling off such a massive theft was short-lived, however. Although they all disappeared to various haunts, it did not take the police long to track down the farmhouse. A broken contract by a fellow villain to sweep the place clean meant the gang's fingerprints were everywhere. Soon the Great Train Robbers' faces were on 'Wanted' posters throughout Britain.

Within a year, most were behind bars. Gang members Gordon Goody, Bob Welch, Roy James,

Tommy Wisbey and Jim Hussey all got 30 years, though they were released after serving 12 of them. Roger Cordrey was sentenced to 14 years and served seven. Jimmy White was sentenced to 18 years and served nine. Buster Edwards, who eventually gave himself up, was later released after serving nine years of a 15-year sentence. Charlie Wilson was sentenced to 30 years, broke out of jail in 1964, but was arrested in Canada three years later. And Bruce Reynolds, reckoned to be a mastermind of the gang, was arrested in Torquay, Devon, in 1968 and sentenced to 25 years.

Things must have looked pretty bleak, too, for Ronnie Biggs. He had stood in the dock and heard his 30-year sentence read out. But as he sat in his prison cell, Ronnie couldn't get the thought of his secret stash of banknotes out of his mind. In July 1965 he was 'sprung' from London's Wandsworth Prison by a gang of nimble-footed, daredevil associates. Ronnie scaled the wall and jumped on to the roof of a waiting furniture van.

Determined no one would recognise him wherever he went, Ronnie's first port of call was France, where he had plastic surgery to his nose and cheekbones. He then packed up his stashed-away share of the Great Train Robbery haul and high-tailed it to Australia. Surprisingly, Ronnie did not splash his money about. Instead, he found a job. And there was no high living, with Ronnie working by day as a carpenter and returning for quiet evenings at home with wife Charmian and their three sons. They only made one major change in their lives: adopting new names.

It could have been an everlasting, idyllic existence but for two events. The first was the death of their eldest son in a car crash, the second a tip-off that Scotland Yard were in hot pursuit. Charmian and Ronnie decided she and her sons would stay in Australia while he fled to Brazil. It was a decision Charmian was to regret.

With his charming smile and sense of humour, Ronnie soon became a well-known character in Rio de Janeiro. Deep down, however, he missed his wife and family. Loneliness led him into a sensational life of drink, drugs and women.

In 1994, a reporter from a London newspaper tracked Ronnie down to write his life story – but the reporter's bosses felt obliged to tip off Scotland Yard about their exclusive subject. On 1 February 1974 Chief Superintendent Jack Slipper and a fellow police officer arrived to recapture Ronnie.

But ever-lucky, Ronnie escaped the grasp of the law again. No one had told the London policemen that Brazil didn't have an extradition agreement with Britain – and Rio police refused to hand him over.

By now, Ronnie had found a steady relationship with Brazilian girlfriend Raimunda. When she announced she was pregnant, it was more than just impending fatherhood that had Ronnie overjoyed – for, by law, the father of a Brazilian child could not be deported. It was yet another guarantee that Ronnie's rearrest would be forever so near, and yet so far for the British police.

Annoyingly for Ronnie, he did find himself back in prison in 1981. But it was a gang of kidnappers, not the law, who got their hands on him. Former British Army sergeant John Miller and four other men befriended Ronnie in Rio.

Ronnie had no reason to suspect their motives and, having split from Raimunda, he enjoyed the company. One night outside a Copacabana bar, the gang grabbed him, put a gag on him and pushed him inside a sack. Ronnie was smuggled out of the country, eventually arriving by yacht in the Caribbean. Miller wanted to sell the last of the Great Train Robbers to the highest bidder.

But the yacht on which Ronnie was being held broke down and was seized by coastguards as it drifted into Barbados' waters. The kidnappers escaped, leaving poor Ronnie to be throw into jail to await extradition to Britain.

Back at Scotland Yard, police teams rubbed their hands with glee. At last, they thought, Ronnie's charmed life was coming to end.

It was not to be. Ronnie's best mates in Rio,

cockney John Pickston and his Brazilian wife Lia, hired top lawyer Ezra Alleyne. After three weeks of clever legal wrangling, the Chief Justice of Barbados, Sir William Douglas, ruled that the extradition treaty between the island and Britain was not valid. Ronnie was walking free again...with £30,000 for the costs of his case.

Biggs strode out of the courtroom into the brilliant sunshine, to be greeted by a welcome crowd of cheering islanders. 'Champagne for everyone', he shouted. 'The drinks are on me!'

Ronnie Biggs returned to Brazil a celebrity. His son Mike brought Ronnie additional reflected glory when he grew up to become a pop musician. And every British journalist passing through Rio would call on the Biggs' home for a cheery quote. On a beachside bar at Copacabana any evening, a silver-haired expatriate might be seen sipping an iced drink and reflecting on the possibility that sometimes, just sometimes, crime can be made to pay.

But, in reality, this was not to be the case for Ronnie Biggs. As he says ruefully:

'After 30 years people still ask me how much I have left from the Great Train Robbery. Some smirk when I reply that my share had gone after only three years – but it's true. A third of the money went on my escape from Wandsworth Prison to Australia, a lot was ripped off by my minders, and I gave a lot away to family and friends – which I don't regret. So don't go looking for buried treasure because there isn't any. Otherwise, why would I still be hustling "I Met Ronnie Biggs" T-shirts to British tourists?'

CRIME DOESN'T PAY!

If this book has made you think that crime is just fine – forget it! Crime may often sound an attractive prospect but that doesn't mean it's all fun – as the following stories of bungling burglars, hold-up horrors and con-artist cock-ups show.

Take, for instance, the story of the greatest police 'sting' of all time. It was pulled in the industrial town of Flint, Michigan.

No crook likes it when they try to pull off a sting and get stung themselves. But undercover cops pride themselves on outsmarting villains – as the following stories show.

The snappiest work by crime-fighters in the United States was at the funeral of a local Mr Big known as 'Lucky' in Flint, Michigan.

The deceased had been a well-known 'fence' – a handler of stolen property. His early demise meant that police were thwarted in bringing him to justice, so they settled for his friends instead. Their task was made easy when 60 of Lucky's gang arrived in church to pay their last respects. The Sting Squad swept into action and rounded up every single one of the villains, who were responsible for handling approximately $1 million of other people's property.

But there was even worse news for that particular

criminal fraternity. With the skill of the squad's own Mr Big – 40-year-old Walter Ryerson, Treasury Department investigator – another staggering total of 300 crooks were later arrested. Ryerson had master-minded both operations, previously spending months undercover infiltrating the gang. He even managed to video his business transactions. As one villain was to say later: 'You just don't know who you can trust these days'.

Perhaps the contemporary film *The Sting* best sums up the work of clever con men. The movie has Robert Redford and Paul Newman as two tricksters who cheated a gangland boss out of a fortune in a gambling house.

Ironically, although a bit of fictional fun, the film provided the United States' real-life police forces with an intriguing insight into the minds of crooks.

Not long after the film's release in 1976, federal agents in California embarked on their own sting. They set up seven warehouses, which were to be used for receiving stolen goods.

The cops then entered the criminal world, posing as fences, buying up every single 'hot' haul they were offered. They dealt in anything, from jewellery and guns to stolen vehicles.

Over 200 arrests were finally made. Most of these came about when the undercover cops invited the thieves to attend parties to celebrate their successful villainy. One guest was a particularly nasty hit-man who offered his services to the cop 'criminals' in case they wanted to get rid of unwanted underworld rivals. And in all, property worth millions of dollars was recovered, stolen from throughout the Los Angeles area.

Sting Squads became commonplace in playing crooks at their own game, with hundreds of crime bosses ending up behind bars. Less dramatic, perhaps, were some of the other occasions when crime was proved NOT to pay.

Perhaps the ultimate story of the crook who realised that crime is not worthwhile is the tale of the bandit who walked into a bank in Davenport, Tasmania, put a bag on the counter and told the girl teller: 'Fill it up – I've got a gun'.

The girl started to empty the tellers' tills until the robber stopped her at $5,000 and told her: 'That's enough for me.'

Minutes later he reappeared, put the loot back on the counter and told the girl: 'Sorry, miss, I didn't really want to rob you.' Then he calmly waited for the police to arrive.

Another would-be bandit handed a bank cashier in Delray Beach, Florida, a badly-spelled note which read: 'I got a bum. I can blow you sky high.' The cashier showed it to his colleagues and they all fell about laughing. The would-be thief was so embarrassed that he ran away.

After robbing a garage in Reno, Nevada, a gunman allowed the owner to make just one phone call. He did – to the police.

Finding that his unfortunate victim had no cash, a mugger in Essex, England, forced him to write out a cheque. 'My name is Andrew Cross – make it out to me', he ordered.

His victim promptly went to the police, armed with the name of his assailant.

A policeman was amazed when a thief waved at him from the Bristol shop he was burgling. The crook had mistaken the officer for his accomplice.

During a chase after a burglar in the same city, a policeman yelled: 'Stop thief!' But the man kept on running. So the constable tried imitating a snarling police dog – and the youth stopped in his tracks and gave himself up.

A bank robber at Portland, Oregon, handed a cashier a slip of paper which read: 'This is a hold-up and I've got a gun.' The cashier gave a nod and waited while the man scribbled another note: 'Put all your money in a paper bag', and handed it across the counter. Turning the note over, the cashier wrote: 'I don't have a paper bag.' The man ran off.

A burglar broke into what he thought was an apartment block and found himself in the hands of the law – right inside Knightsbridge Magistrates'

Court, London.

Hoping to cut his electricity bills, a County Tyrone man tampered with his meter. But unluckily for him, the Irishman had fiddled it in the electricity board's favour and clocked up thousands of extra units and a bill for £400.

Two raiders, out to rob a post office in Buckinghamshire, tricked the postmistress into opening the security window by asking her to change two £50 notes.

She snatched their money and slammed the window shut. They fled, not only empty-handed, but £100 worse off.

In a similar blunder by a burglar in the same locality, the crook, who was planning to raid a wine shop, broke into the wrong store, took nothing, was arrested within minutes and then suffered the indignity of a judge telling him: 'Give up crime, you're no good at it.'

Another wine shop raid that went wrong for the villain took place in Yorkshire.

When the robber pushed a note demanding cash across the counter, shopkeeper John Peterson had to laugh. Neatly printed at the top was the man's name and address.

When the thief produced what appeared to be a gun in a handkerchief, 'Have-a-go Hero' Peterson pelted him with sweets from a jar, then chased him out of the shop armed with a bottle of Coca Cola. Local detectives caught up with the hapless thief an hour later.

Robbers used too much explosive on a bank safe in Munkebo, Denmark, and demolished the building. When they finally managed to crawl out they found the safe still intact.

Police soon caught up with a thieving motorist who drove off without paying from petrol station in the English Midlands – and spluttered to a halt less than half a mile up the road. He phoned for a rescue crew from the Automobile Association who soon diagnosed the problem. The thief had filled up with diesel fuel instead of petrol.

Two students convicted of siphoning three gallons of petrol from a car in North Carolina, got four miles to the gallon. They were sentenced to walk 12 miles.

A freckle-faced nine-year-old boy faced a New York court in 1981 charged with being the United States' youngest bank robber.

He had walked into a bank, pulled out a toy pistol, held up a teller and walked out with $100 – having been totally undetected by the security cameras because he was so small!

The little menace blew his haul on hamburgers, French fries, candies and a watch that played a tune. Then he turned himself in.

The 75 convicts who tunnelled out of a jail at

Saltillo, in northern Mexico, slipped up on the planning. After six months of hard digging for freedom, they emerged in the nearby courtroom where most of them had been sentenced to time behind bars.

Forgers are often caught by their printing mistakes. But a Kenyan crook who produced near-perfect banknotes was easily identified, thanks to his vanity. Instead of a portrait of the president, he used a picture of himself.

In England, two handcuffed prisoners leapt from a prison van in Luton, Bedfordshire, and made a dash for freedom. But the shackled pair were stopped short when they ran past a lamp-post, one on either side of it. They were yanked off their feet, collided in mid-air and crashed to the ground in agony. They were rushed to hospital suffering from dislocated arms and crushed ribs.

Two lovers running drugs for a gang discussed their mission as they cuddled in a Worcestershire hotel room – not realising the baby alarm was on and everything they said was being broadcast to the reception desk.

The receptionist immediately summoned the police.

Three prisoners from Lincoln were hitching a lift when a bus stopped for them – and out jumped seven warders from their jail who recaptured them. The 'bus' contained a prison party on its way to court.

An armed man barged to the front of the queue in a Texas bank and shouted: 'This is a stick-up. Give me the money!'

The 20-year-old cashier retorted firmly: 'You're in the wrong line. Wait over there.' The raider meekly did as he was told until the police turned up.

Nothing went right when an Italian decided to rob a bank in Milan. He tripped on a doormat as he burst in, and fell over.

His mask dropped from his face and his revolver accidentally went off. He got up, ran towards a cashier and slipped over again, grabbing the counter to get his balance.

His gun fell to the floor. With staff and customers laughing at his bungling, the humiliated thief decided to make his exit. He ran out of the door and collided with a policeman who was standing on the pavement writing out a traffic ticket for his illegally-parked getaway car.

A thief broke into a London electrical shop to steal television sets but drove off with three microwave ovens by mistake. In court, the judge suspended the man's 18-month jail sentence because of his 'crass stupidity'.

A cool Southampton crook strolled into a city supermarket and filled a basket with goods. He gave the check-out girl a £10 note, intending to snatch the contents of the opened till. But it contained only £4.37, which he nevertheless took – losing £5.63 on his criminal shopping spree.

A hapless hold-up merchant disguised his identity by placing a pillowcase over his head and dashed into a store in Riverside, California.

After crashing into several display counters, the bandit realised that he should have cut eye-holes in the mask. He raised the pillowcase to find his way out of the store, was recognised by a customer and later arrested.

A pretty, pregnant girl of 27 won the sympathy of the court when she appeared before magistrates at Malmo, Sweden, charged with shoplifting. They leniently placed her on probation. As she left the court smiling, police again pounced on her and dragged her back – to be charged with walking out wearing a fur coat belonging to one of the magistrates.

A customs officer sauntered up to a truck that had just driven off an English Channel ferry at Dover. Knocking on the side of it, he shouted: 'Are you all right in there?' Back came the reply from 22 Asian illegal immigrants: 'Yes!'

A man charged with purse-snatching in Tulsa, Oklahoma, denied the charge and opted to present his own defence. He began by asking a woman victim: 'Did you get a good look at my face when I grabbed your bag?...Err...'. He was immediately found guilty and jailed.

A man bought a cheap imitation revolver, pulled a pair of ladies' tights over his head and burst into a jewellery store in Liverpool, shouting: 'This is a stick-up. Get down.'

No one moved – for the raider had forgotten to take the cork out of the barrel of the pistol. In a rage, the robber fled, tearing off his mask. He was instantly recognised by the jewellery shop owner and was later arrested and jailed.

A gunman who robbed a Paris grocery store lost his hat as he ran away. Written inside were his name and address, and police were waiting for him when he got home.

A Denver bandit crashed his getaway car into a lamp post but escaped on foot.

Arriving home, however, he fumbled for his latch key while still holding his gun – and shot himself in the leg.

A German shoplifter trying to evade pursuing police shinned down a drainpipe and landed in the exercise yard of Dusseldorf jail. Six stolen watches were found in his pockets, and the bungling thief ended up doing time.

Two British burglars came across a camera in the house they were raiding and, for fun, took photographs of each other with their loot.

Unfortunately for them, they dropped the camera as they made their escape, and police returned it to its owner, a 75-year-old Tyneside woman. Three months later she had the film developed, and the two raiders were swiftly identified and arrested.

A mugger on the tourist island of Majorca tried to snatch the handbags of two German great-grandmothers, both aged 77. They overpowered him, locked him in the boot of their car and drove him to a police station.

A bungling British burglar broke into an apartment in Chester but could not get out again. Not even an axe would open the now-jammed door. He resignedly opened a bottle of stolen Scotch and waited for the owner to return home and turn him in.

Safebreakers in England's West Midlands tried to cut through a metal door with an oxy-acetylene torch. Unfamiliar with the device, they failed to turn up the oxygen supply and consequently spent hours cutting a hole large enough to put a hand through. Only after they were captured and brought to court did they learn that the safe door had not even been locked.

Fifteen Asians who waded ashore at Hallandale, Florida, dressed in dark three-piece suits and carrying briefcases were arrested as illegal immigrants. The Asians, who had travelled from Bombay via the Caribbean, believed that their 'disguises' would help them blend with the locals. Unfortunately for them, according to a police spokesman: 'They kinda stood out in the surf at 3.30 am.'

After snatching a television set from a Glasgow store, a thief made off pushing his friend, who was holding the loot, in a wheelchair. They managed to get only 400 metres before police caught up with them.

A burglar stole a budgerigar in a raid on a house in Rochdale, Lancashire, because he thought his own budgerigar needed some company. But the stolen budgie, called Peter, got his own back by 'shopping' the burglar to the police. When detectives visited the raider's home, Peter was able to identify himself by giving his name – and a good impression of the owner's ringing telephone.

Armed with a toy revolver and wearing a full-face crash helmet as a mask, a man relieved a 15-year-old Yorkshire shop assistant of £157.

He was soon traced to his Scarborough home, thanks to his crash helmet, which bore his name in inch-high letters.

Also in the same county, a burglar with one leg, one eye and a withered hand was urged by magistrates to swop his career of crime for 'a more rewarding occupation' when he received his seventh conviction in 1977.

A burglar trying to make a getaway after setting off the alarm in a do-it-yourself store in Chesterfield,

Derbyshire, was faced with a choice of twelve doors, each complete with brasswork and hinges. But they transpired to be display models, each opening onto a blank wall. After trying them all in darkness, the man climbed a staircase, only to fall back down, knocking himself out.

A man and a woman were arrested for fare dodging by transport police in New York when they tried to get a free ride. The bus they chose was carrying 75 people to court, all about to be charged with fare dodging.

Several months after her car had been stolen, a Manchester woman hired a taxi to take her to a dinner dance.

Halfway there she realised from a mark on the upholstery that she was sitting in her own car.

Gunmen burst into a Plymouth betting shop shouting: 'This is a hold-up. Freeze!' They fled after being totally ignored by the punters, who were intently listening to a race report.

Three men who stole 31 rainbow trout owned by a Mr Herring were caught by police led by Superintendent Pike.

When a gunman thrust a demand note at her, a Chinese girl teller in a Vancouver bank asked him in English: 'What do you want?' The raider replied: 'All your money.'

Confused, the girl called over another teller who

asked the man what he wanted in French. He replied in French but his English accent was so strong that the tellers had to call in the manager for help. The manager looked blankly at the note and explained in French that he couldn't speak English. At this point the robber gave up.

A man arrested after being seen crawling along the roof of a London-Birmingham train said: 'I had a second-class ticket and was trying to get to the bar.'

A driver in Oklahoma City was fined for being drunk in charge of a car and of stealing a horse, which was found sitting beside him in the passenger seat at the time of the arrest.

The quiet of a United States' transcontinental jet flight was disturbed in 1976 by a passenger who seized an air stewardess and demanded: 'Take this plane to Detroit'. When the cabin crew member explained to him that the plane was already going to Detroit, he sat down again.

A man accused of stealing a chewing gum machine from outside a Philadelphia store was ordered by the court to chew all 250 packets of gum in the machine.

Thieves who raided a home at Tooting, London, stole two dozen sealed bags. Police never recovered the bags but they do not believe the raiders enjoyed their haul. The bags contained hundreds of thousands of fleas.

And as a final epitaph to the notion that crime **can**

pay, a gravestone in a churchyard in Sheldon, Vermont, bears this legend to an unknown burglar, shot while robbing a store on 13 October 1905:

HERE LIES A BURGLAR
*This stone was bought
with money found on him*